# From my Oven

*Fay Lewis*

This book is dedicated to the special girls in my life, my daughters Tamara, Marissa and Carmen, and to my husband Leon, without whom I wouldn't have such talented daughters.

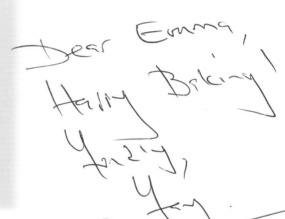

*Dear Emma,*
*Happy Baking!*
*Yours,*
*Fay.*

# From my Oven

*Fay Lewis*

Photography by Neil Corder

Project co-ordination by Justine Kiggen

Food and décor styling by Lisa Clark

First published in 2007 by Struik Publishers (a division of New Holland Publishing (South Africa) (Pty) Ltd)

New Holland Publishing is a member of Avusa Ltd

Cornelis Struik House, 80 McKenzie Street, Cape Town 8001

86–88 Edgware Road, London, W2 2EA, United Kingdom

Unit 1, 66 Gibbes Street, Chatswood, NSW 2067, Australia

218 Lake Road, Northcote, Auckland, New Zealand

**www.struik.co.za**

**PUBLISHING MANAGER:** Linda de Villiers
**MANAGING EDITOR:** Cecilia Barfield
**EDITOR:** Irma van Wyk
**DESIGNER:** Helen Henn
**PHOTOGRAPHER:** Neil Corder
**PROJECT CO-ORDINATOR:** Justine Kiggen
**FOOD AND DÉCOR STYLIST:** Lisa Clark
**PROOFREADER AND INDEXER:** Joy Clack

ISBN 978 1 77007 564 1

Reproduction by Hirt & Carter Cape

Printed and bound by Craft Print International Ltd, Singapore

www.imagesofafrica.co.za
IMAGES OF AFRICA
PHOTO LIBRARY

Over 40 000 unique African images available to purchase from our image bank at www.imagesofafrica.co.za

I owe particular thanks to Linda de Villiers (Publishing Manager) for compiling the detailed content and for your encouragement, advice and support throughout the writing of it. Your devotion to the task at hand and your incredible work ethic are an inspiration to us all.

I record my thanks to Irma van Wyk (Senior Editor) for your quiet professionalism in editing the manuscript with such care and for your unfailing interest in this book from start to finish.

My sincerest gratitude to Helen Henn (Senior Designer) for your guiding hand in creating the original layouts with such panache and for your conscientious input at so many of the photographic shoots.

Nelani Pfaff (Senior Editor) for your commitment and time spent in editing the Afrikaans manuscript.

Neil Corder (Photographer), a true gentleman, for your superlative photography and endless patience.

Justine Kiggen (Project Co-ordinator) for conscientiously attending to every detail in such a loving and professional manner.

Lisa Clark (Food and Décor Stylist) for your artistic flair, special touch and completely original presentation.

Raphaella Frame (Food Preparation) for preparing the food with such loving care and attention to detail.

Melissa Kirchner (Digital Photographic Assistant) for willingly attending to every task at hand.

Tessa Holding (Décor Stylist's Assistant) for assisting and pre-empting all our needs.

Lizette Baker (Prop Sourcing) for our many photographic shoots.

I wish to thank Naomie Blom, Eric and Rona Ellerine, Martin Ellert, Shereen Fihrer, Mimi Jossel, Janine Lazarus and Ita Stern for all their support and encouragement.

The author and publishers also wish to thank the following persons and companies for their kind assistance and/ or loan of props for the photography:

Uwe Sherman of Thrupps; Wally Clack and Dalene van Niekerk of Gideon's Flowers and Functions; Glenda of the Patisserie, Illovo; Wendy of Cottage Flowers, Hyde Park; Kay and Lynn of Bunches, Parktown North; the management of Head Interiors; Lauren Abelheim of Apsley House; Margaret at House & Interiors, Cavendish Square; Peggy and Ann at Peggy's Place and Plate Hiring, Diep River.

# Contents

# Introduction

My love for baking started at a young age as I sat cross-legged on my mom's kitchen table, licking away at the bowl of delicious batter!

Baking is an exact science and, although it is often challenging, it is certainly not daunting. These recipes, from the most simple to the more complicated, will fill you with pride once you have prepared them.

I particularly enjoy baking because:

- The kitchen remains 'clean' – there is nothing that gets really dirty or greasy!
- The ingredients are easy to acquire and most economical – a bag of cake flour goes a long way!
- I find it very necessary to concentrate whilst baking, hence nobody may interrupt me!
- The home-baked product always tastes so much better than the store-bought version.
- Your home is filled with the heavenly aroma of sweet, baked goodies ....

## Baking Techniques

The recipes in this book were tested in an electric thermo fan oven.

None of the recipes are suitable for baking in a microwave or microwave/convection oven.

The oven rack and cake tins were positioned so that the top of the baked product was more or less in the centre of the oven.

All the dry ingredients were accurately weighed on a gram scale. For ease of reference, however, measurements in millilitres have also been included in brackets in some instances. Measurements are always level.

Butter or hard baking margarine was used in the testing process. If baking with margarine, you will trade the distinctive flavour that only butter provides!

## Five different sugars were used:

White sugar
Golden brown sugar (light yellow in colour)
Caramel brown sugar (dark brown in colour)
Castor sugar
Icing sugar

Jumbo eggs at room temperature were used in the testing process.

Unless otherwise specified, water at room temperature was used in the recipes.

All baking tins, irrespective of specified preparation, should be sprayed with cooking spray.

loaf tins

cutters

French flan, sifter

mixing bowl, balloon whisk

food mixer

wire rack, madeleine, tube tin

Bundt tins, swiss roll tin

scale, baking beans

square tin, springform tin

tart tin, round cake tin

grater

piping bag and nozzles

wooden spoon,
rolling pin, pastry brush

food processor

metal spoon, spatula, palette knife

baking tray, giant muffin tin

measuring cups and spoons

rectangular and brioche tins

## Preparing Baking Tins

### Step-by-step to lining a deep square tin with baking paper

1. Place the tin in the centre of a square of baking paper and, using a sharp knife or the blade of a pair of scissors, draw around the base. Cut out as marked.

2. Cut a strip of baking paper the same depth as the sides of the tin and long enough to cover all four sides.

3. Place the square of paper in the base of the tin.

4. Position the strip around the inside of the tin.

### Lining round tins with baking paper

Place the tin on a square of baking paper, draw around it using a sharp knife and cut out as marked. Place in the base of the tin. Cut a strip of baking paper the same depth as the side of the tin and long enough to cover the inside. Position the strip around the inside of the tin.

# Preparing Pastry Tins

## Step-by-step to lining a French flan tin with pastry

1. Roll out the pastry to a circle 4 cm wider than the diameter of the tin.
2. Using the rolling pin, lift the pastry, centre it over the tin and ease it into place.
3. Working from the centre outwards, press the pastry into the flan tin so that it fits snugly into the bottom edge and up the sides.
4. Roll the rolling pin across the rim of the tin to remove excess pastry.
5. Press around the rim and into the fluted sides with the fingertips.
6. Using a fork, prick the base in several places to release any trapped air and to help prevent rising during cooking.
7. Place in the freezer for 10 minutes, then remove. This will make the pastry firmer.

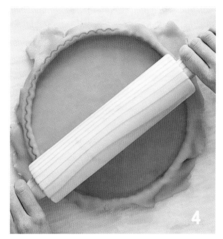

## Step-by-step to baking blind

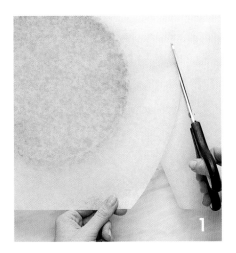

1 Cut a circle of baking paper about 10 cm larger than the diameter of the baking tin.
2 Place the baking paper circle in the pastry-lined tin.
3 Weigh the baking paper down with a layer of uncooked dried beans or uncooked rice.
4 Place the tin on a baking sheet.
5 Bake in a preheated oven at 200 °C for 10 minutes. Remove from the oven.

6 Carefully lift out the baking paper and beans. If the pastry is 'soggy' to the touch, bake for an extra 5 minutes without the paper and beans.

# On the Rise

*These crusty creations will keep you satisfied throughout the day.*

## Yeast Basics

- Read the recipe thoroughly before starting to bake, and weigh and measure all the ingredients accurately. Ensure all equipment and ingredients are on hand.
- 25 g **fresh yeast** is equivalent to 10 g **instant dry yeast**.
- Always use the specified flour. **Cake flour** is the most refined flour and **white bread flour** is most commonly used for all types of white bread. **Brown bread flour** gives the same texture as white bread flour, but the colour is different because of the amount of bran present. **Wholewheat flour** produces a coarser and darker baked product owing to the high percentage of bran and wheat germ in the flour.
- All **liquids** used in bread making must be lukewarm. If the liquid is cold the yeast activity will be slow and, if the liquid is too hot, the yeast cells will be destroyed.
- **Salt** in yeast baking improves the flavour.
- **Sugar** acts as a source of food for the yeast and sweetens the baked product.
- **Butter** or **margarine** enhances the flavour of the baked product and increases the elasticity of the dough.
- **Eggs** are added in yeast baking for a richer flavour and colour, and also to enhance the texture of the baked product.
- If **fruit** is added, do so after the first rising and before shaping the dough.

## *Working with Yeast*

### Tips for Yeast Baking

- **Fresh yeast** becomes active in the presence of moisture (lukewarm water), food (sugar) and warmth. Once the yeast is active, carbon dioxide is produced and acts as the raising agent. When the fresh yeast becomes active add it to the dry ingredients and the remaining liquid, and mix until a soft but not sticky dough is formed. If the dough is too sticky, add a little extra flour.
- **Instant dry yeast** needs no hydration and is mixed directly into the dry ingredients. The liquid is added to form a dough.
- Never cut short the **kneading** time, as it will affect the texture of the bread. Kneading is essential to distribute the yeast and to develop the gluten in the flour. Knead for at least 10 minutes by hand or for 5 minutes if using a food mixer fitted with the dough hook.
- Once the dough has been kneaded, set aside in a large bowl covered with clingfilm and leave in a warm place to **rise** until doubled in size. Fresh yeast will take about 45 minutes while instant dry yeast will take 20–25 minutes to activate.
- Once the dough has risen, **knock down** the dough to release all the carbon dioxide produced by the yeast. For a finer texture leave the dough to rise for a second time and then knock down again.
- **Shape** the dough as per the recipe instruction, cover with clingfilm and set aside at room temperature to **prove** until doubled in size. Proving time takes 20–45 minutes.
- Prepare the dough for **baking** as per the recipe instruction. Once the bread is baked, test for doneness by tapping the base of the bread with the knuckles – the bread must sound hollow – or until a skewer inserted into the centre comes out clean.
- Remove from the oven and leave to **cool** in the tin for 10 minutes. Turn out onto a wire rack to cool.

# Traditional White Bread

Makes 1 loaf

400 ml lukewarm water

1 x 10 g packet instant dry yeast

5 ml sugar

700 g (5 x 250 ml) white bread flour

15 ml salt

25 ml butter or margarine

30 ml water

Preheat the oven to 200 °C.

Coat a 28 x 11 cm loaf tin with cooking spray and set aside.

1 Pour the 400 ml water into a bowl, sprinkle the yeast and sugar over and set aside for 10 minutes until frothy.

2 Sift the flour and salt into a large mixing bowl.

3 Rub in the butter or margarine until the mixture resembles breadcrumbs.

4 Make a well in the centre of the mixture and pour in the yeast liquid. Using a wooden spoon, draw the flour into the liquid to form a dough. Mix thoroughly.

5 Turn the dough out onto a lightly floured surface and knead for 10 minutes or until the dough is smooth and pliable.

6 Shape the dough into a ball, place into a large bowl, cover with clingfilm and set aside in a warm place to rise until the dough has doubled in size.

7 Turn the dough out onto a lightly floured surface and punch down to remove any air bubbles.

8 Return the dough to the bowl, cover with clingfilm again and set aside in a warm place to rise until doubled in size.

9 Shape the dough into the prepared tin, cover with clingfilm and set aside in a warm place to prove.

10 Remove the clingfilm and brush the top of the dough with the 30 ml water.

11 Bake for 45 minutes or until a skewer inserted into the centre comes out clean and the bread sounds hollow when tapped with the knuckles.

12 Remove from the oven and leave to cool in the tin for 10 minutes. Turn out onto a wire rack to cool.

**Handy hint**

If the dough is too dry, it can be a problem adding more water at the end of mixing. To avoid this, wet the hands frequently during the first stages of kneading.

# Traditional Brown Bread

**Traditional Brown Bread** is made in exactly the same way as Traditional White Bread.
Simply substitute the 700 g white bread flour with 700 g brown bread flour and add an extra 25 ml butter or margarine.

# Moist Wholewheat Bread

Makes 1 loaf

375 ml water

80 ml golden syrup

80 g butter or margarine

280 g (500 ml) cake flour

10 ml salt

280 g wholewheat flour

80 g (250 ml) oats

30 g (250 ml) digestive bran

1 x 10 g packet instant dry yeast

25 ml milk

50 ml raw linseeds

Preheat the oven to 180 °C.

Coat a 28 x 11 cm loaf tin (or two smaller tins) with cooking spray and set aside. Heat the water, syrup and butter or margarine in the microwave at 100% power for 90 seconds and set aside to cool until lukewarm. Sift the cake flour and salt into a large mixing bowl. Add the wholewheat flour, oats and bran, and mix. Make a well in the centre and add the yeast and the water mixture. Mix thoroughly and spoon into the prepared tin. Cover with clingfilm and set aside in a warm place to prove. Remove the clingfilm, brush the top of the dough with the milk and sprinkle with the linseeds. Bake for 55 minutes until golden brown in colour or until a skewer inserted into the centre comes out clean. Remove from the oven and leave to cool in the tin for 10 minutes. Turn out onto a wire rack to cool.

# Special Wholewheat Bread

Makes 2 loaves

400 ml lukewarm water

100 ml honey

2 x 10 g packets instant dry yeast

1 kg wholewheat flour

20 ml salt

60 g (100 ml) sunflower seeds

70 g (100 ml) raw linseeds or sesame seeds

600 ml lukewarm water

Preheat the oven to 200 °C.

Coat two 28 x 11 cm loaf tins with cooking spray and set aside. Combine the 400 ml water and honey in a bowl, sprinkle the yeast over and set aside for 10 minutes until frothy. Mix the flour, salt and seeds in a large mixing bowl and pour in the yeast mixture and 600 ml water. Using a wooden spoon, draw the flour into the yeast liquid to form a dough. Mix thoroughly until the dough is soft and sticky. Spoon the dough into the prepared tins, cover with clingfilm and set aside in a warm place to prove. Remove the clingfilm and bake for 45 minutes or until a skewer inserted into the centre comes out clean and the loaves sound hollow when tapped with the knuckles. Remove from the oven and leave to cool in the tins for 10 minutes, then turn out onto a wire rack to cool.

# French Bread

Makes 2 loaves

900 g cake flour

20 ml salt

15 ml sugar

1 x 10 g packet instant dry yeast

25 ml butter or margarine

600 ml lukewarm water

50 ml water

Preheat the oven to 220 °C.

Coat two baking sheets with cooking spray and set aside.

1   Mix the flour, salt and sugar in a large mixing bowl and stir in the yeast.

2   Rub in the butter or margarine with the fingertips.

3   Add the 600 ml water and mix thoroughly to form a soft dough.

4   Knead the dough in the bowl until smooth and pliable.

5   Turn the dough out onto a lightly floured surface and knead for 10 minutes or until the dough is smooth and elastic.

6   Shape the dough into a ball, place into a large bowl, cover with clingfilm and set aside in a warm place to rise until the dough has doubled in size.

7   Turn the dough out onto the lightly floured surface again and punch down to remove any air bubbles.

8   Divide the dough into two equal pieces and shape into loaves. Place onto the prepared sheets and make diagonal cuts along the top of each loaf.

9   Cover with clingfilm and set aside in a warm place to prove.

10  Remove the clingfilm and brush the top of each loaf with the 50 ml water.

11  Bake for 25 minutes or until a skewer inserted into the centre comes out clean and the bread sounds hollow when tapped with the knuckles.

12  Remove from the oven and leave to cool on the baking sheets for 10 minutes, then place onto a cooling rack to cool.

**Handy hint**

To ensure a crisp crust, fill a roasting pan with boiling water and place it on the floor of the oven prior to baking the bread.

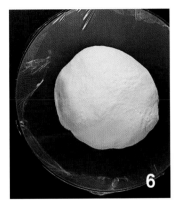

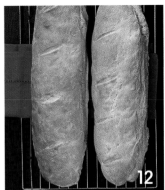

# Rye Bread

Makes 2 loaves

400 g brown rye flour

600 g white bread flour

20 ml salt

25 ml caraway seeds

1 x 10 g packet instant dry yeast

40 ml butter or margarine

20 ml molasses

15 ml liquid glucose

600 ml lukewarm water

Preheat the oven to 200 °C.

Coat two baking sheets with cooking spray and set aside. Sift the flours and salt into a large mixing bowl, stir in the seeds and the yeast, and mix. Rub in the butter or margarine, then add the molasses, glucose and water, and mix thoroughly to form a soft dough. Knead the dough in the bowl until smooth and pliable. Turn the dough out onto a lightly floured surface and knead for 10 minutes or until the dough is even more smooth and pliable. Shape the dough into a ball, place into a large bowl, cover with clingfilm and set aside in a warm place to rise until the dough has doubled in size. Turn the dough out onto the lightly floured surface again and punch down to remove any air bubbles.

Divide the dough into two equal pieces and shape into two round or torpedo-shaped loaves. Place the loaves onto the prepared sheets and make a few diagonal cuts along the top of each loaf. Cover with clingfilm and set aside in a warm place to prove. Remove the clingfilm and bake for 35 minutes or until a skewer inserted into the centre comes out clean and the bread sounds hollow when tapped with the knuckles. Remove from the oven and leave to cool on the baking sheets for 10 minutes. Place onto a wire rack to cool.

# Kitke or Challah

Makes 1 large loaf

50 ml butter, melted

550 g white bread flour, sifted

125 ml lukewarm water

80 g (100 ml) sugar

100 ml lukewarm milk or
      apple juice

2 jumbo eggs, beaten

3 jumbo egg yolks, beaten

10 ml coarse salt

1 x 10 g packet instant dry yeast

50 ml butter, melted

**Coating**

1 jumbo egg, beaten with 50 ml melted
      butter or margarine for egg wash

80 g (100 ml) sugar

75 ml cake flour

30 ml cooking oil

Preheat the oven to 190 °C.

Coat a baking sheet with cooking spray and set aside. Brush a large mixing bowl with 50 ml melted butter and set aside. Combine all the ingredients in a large mixing bowl and mix thoroughly to form a soft dough. Knead the dough in the bowl until smooth and pliable. Transfer the dough to the butter-coated bowl and cover with clingfilm. Set aside in a warm place to rise until the dough has doubled in size. Remove the clingfilm and knead for 5 minutes or until smooth and elastic. Brush the top of the dough with the other 50 ml melted butter and again cover with clingfilm. Set aside in a warm place to rise until doubled in size.

Remove the clingfilm and divide the dough into three equal pieces. Roll each piece into a ball and place on a lightly floured surface. Cover with clingfilm and set aside in a warm place to rise for 20 minutes. Remove the clingfilm and roll each ball into a 30 cm 'rope', leaving the middle a little thicker than the ends. Lay the 'ropes' side by side lengthwise, pinching together the ends at the farthest end, and plait the 'ropes'. Pinch the ends together and transfer the kitke to the prepared baking sheet. Brush the kitke with the egg wash. Combine the sugar, flour and oil in a small bowl and sprinkle on top. Cover with clingfilm and set aside in a warm place to prove. Remove the clingfilm and bake for 35–40 minutes or until a skewer inserted into the centre comes out clean. If the kitke browns too quickly, loosely tent with foil. Remove from the oven and leave to cool on the baking sheet for 10 minutes. Turn out onto a wire rack to cool for at least 1 hour before serving.

# Traditional Potbread

Makes 1 loaf

1 kg white bread flour, sifted

30 ml salt

15 ml white sugar

1 x 10 g packet instant dry yeast

80 g butter or margarine

600 ml lukewarm water

1 jumbo egg, beaten

Preheat the oven to 200 °C.

Coat a 33 cm cast-iron pot with cooking spray and set aside. Mix the flour, salt and sugar together in a large mixing bowl and stir in the yeast. Rub in the butter or margarine and add the water. Mix thoroughly to form a soft dough. Knead the dough in the bowl until smooth and pliable. Turn the dough out onto a lightly floured surface, cover with clingfilm and set aside in a warm place to rise for 20 minutes. Remove the clingfilm and punch down the dough to remove any air bubbles. Shape into a ball and place into the prepared pot. Cover with clingfilm and set aside in a warm place to prove for 20–25 minutes. Remove the clingfilm, brush with the egg and bake for 40–45 minutes or until a skewer inserted into the centre comes out clean. Remove from the oven and leave to cool in the pot for 20 minutes. Turn out onto a wire rack to cool.

# Wholewheat Potbread

Makes 1 loaf

1 x 10 g packet instant dry yeast

500 ml lukewarm water

50 ml honey

50 g butter or margarine

10 ml salt

400 g cake flour

350 g wholewheat flour

1 jumbo egg yolk

25 ml milk

50 ml sesame seeds

Preheat the oven to 190 °C.

Coat a 33 cm cast-iron pot with cooking spray and set aside. Dissolve the yeast in the water in a large mixing bowl and set aside until frothy. Add the honey, butter or margarine, salt and flours and, using a wooden spoon, draw the flour mixture into the yeast liquid to form a soft dough. Cover the bowl with clingfilm and set aside in a warm place to rise until doubled in size. Remove the clingfilm and transfer the dough to the prepared pot. Combine the egg yolk and milk and, using a pastry brush, brush the top of the bread with the egg wash. Sprinkle with the sesame seeds and cover the pot with clingfilm. Set aside in a warm place to prove for 20 minutes. Bake for 45 minutes or until a skewer inserted into the centre comes out clean. Remove from the oven and leave to cool in the pot for 20 minutes. Turn out onto a wire rack to cool.

The dough combines in a jiffy in a food mixer fitted with the dough hook.

## Quick Breads

Quick breads contain no yeast; the
dough requires no kneading, rising or
proving before being baked.

# Baby Marrow Bread
Makes 1 loaf

380 g white bread flour

10 ml baking powder

5 ml bicarbonate of soda

10 ml salt

5 ml ground cinnamon

2.5 ml freshly grated nutmeg

1 ml ground cloves

150 g unpeeled baby marrow, grated

160 g (200 ml) golden brown sugar

4 jumbo eggs, beaten

125 ml cooking oil

15 ml grated orange rind

150 g (250 ml) toasted and coarsely chopped
    walnuts or pecan nuts

Preheat the oven to 180 °C.

Coat a 28 x 11 cm loaf tin with cooking spray and set aside. Sift the flour, baking powder, bicarbonate of soda, salt, cinnamon, nutmeg and cloves into a large mixing bowl. Add the baby marrow, sugar, eggs, oil and orange rind, and mix thoroughly. Fold in the nuts. Pour the batter into the prepared tin and bake for 50 minutes or until the edges are browned and start pulling away from the tin, and the bread springs back when lightly pressed with the fingertips. Remove from the oven and leave to cool in the tin for 10 minutes. Turn out onto a wire rack to cool.

# Cornbread

Makes 1 loaf

15 ml butter or margarine

25 ml maize meal

140 g (250 ml) maize meal

140 g (250 ml) cake flour

30 ml white sugar

15 ml baking powder

80 g butter or margarine, melted

2.5 ml salt

2 jumbo eggs, beaten

100 ml milk

1 x 420 g can creamed sweetcorn

Preheat the oven to 180 °C.

Coat a 28 x 11 cm loaf tin with the 15 ml butter or margarine, dust with the 25 ml maize meal and set aside. Mix the rest of the ingredients in a large mixing bowl and stir thoroughly using a wooden spoon to combine. Spoon the batter into the prepared tin and bake for 50 minutes or until a skewer inserted into the centre comes out clean. Remove from the oven and leave to cool in the tin for 10 minutes. Turn out onto a wire rack to cool. Cut into 5 cm square pieces to serve.

This moist bread has a dense texture and the same aroma and flavour of a pumpkin pie. If desired, fold a small handful of chopped walnuts into the batter just before baking.

## Pumpkin Bread
Makes 1 loaf

| | |
|---|---|
| 125 ml boiling water | 1 ml freshly grated nutmeg |
| 75 g (125 ml) seedless raisins | 1 ml ground cloves |
| 180 g cake flour | 250 ml mashed cooked pumpkin |
| 165 g wholewheat flour | 100 g (125 ml) white sugar |
| 5 ml baking powder | 2 jumbo eggs |
| 2.5 ml bicarbonate of soda | 125 ml cooking oil |
| 2.5 ml salt | |
| 2.5 ml ground cinnamon | |

Preheat the oven to 190 °C.

Coat a 21 cm Bundt tin with cooking spray and set aside. Pour the water over the raisins and soak for 10 minutes. Drain and set aside. Sift the flours, baking powder, bicarbonate of soda, salt, cinnamon, nutmeg and cloves into a large mixing bowl. Add the raisins, pumpkin, sugar, eggs and oil and, using a wooden spoon, mix thoroughly to combine. Spoon the batter into the prepared tin. Bake for 35 minutes or until a skewer inserted into the centre comes out with a few moist crumbs and the top and sides are golden brown in colour. Remove from the oven and leave to cool in the tin for 10–15 minutes. Turn out onto a wire rack to cool. Spread with smooth cream cheese at breakfast time or serve for lunch with salad on the side.

# White Bread Rolls

Makes 12

600 g cake flour, sifted

10 ml white sugar

15 ml salt

1 x 10 g packet instant dry yeast

40 ml butter or margarine

100 ml lukewarm milk

2 jumbo eggs, beaten

200 ml lukewarm water

1 jumbo egg, beaten

Preheat the oven to 220 °C.

Coat two baking sheets with cooking spray and set aside.

1  Mix the flour, sugar and salt in a large mixing bowl and add the yeast.

2  Rub in the butter or margarine lightly with the fingertips.

3  Add the milk, eggs and water and mix to form a soft dough.

4  Knead the dough in the bowl until smooth and pliable.

5  Turn the dough out onto a lightly floured surface and knead for 10 minutes or until the dough is smooth and elastic.

6  Shape the dough into a ball, place into a large bowl and cover with clingfilm. Set aside in a warm place to rise until the dough has doubled in size.

7  Turn the dough out onto the lightly floured surface again and punch down to remove any air bubbles.

8  Divide the dough into 12 equal pieces and shape as desired.*

9  Place the bread rolls onto the prepared sheets, brush with the egg wash and cover with clingfilm. Set aside in a warm place to prove for 30 minutes.

10  Remove the clingfilm and bake for 15 minutes or until a skewer inserted into the centre comes out clean.

11  Remove from the oven and leave to cool on the sheets for 5 minutes. Turn out onto a wire rack to cool.

**\* To shape a roll**

Use 40 g of dough per roll to ensure the rolls are all the same size and will bake for the same length of time.

**Dinner rolls**

Roll the dough into a ball 10 cm in diameter and turn the ball over, with the smoothest side uppermost.

**Knots**

Roll the dough into a 10 cm 'rope' and tie into a knot, pinching the ends together.

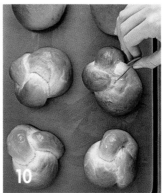

# Wholewheat Rolls

Makes 12

400 g cake flour

400 g wholewheat flour

20 ml caramel brown sugar

15 ml salt

1 x 10 g packet instant dry yeast

25 ml butter or margarine

600 ml lukewarm water

50 ml cold water, for brushing

Preheat the oven to 220 °C.

Follow the method for the Step-by-Step White Bread Rolls up to the end of the shaping of the bread rolls (see page 30).

9   Place the bread rolls onto the prepared sheets, brush with the cold water and cover with clingfilm. Set aside in a warm place to prove for 30 minutes.

10  Remove the clingfilm and bake for 20 minutes or until a skewer inserted into the centre comes out clean.

11  Remove from the oven and leave to cool on the sheets for 5 minutes. Turn out onto a wire rack to cool.

# Bagels
Makes 12

1 kg white bread flour, sifted

20 ml salt

20 ml white sugar

1 x 10 g packet instant dry yeast

20 ml cooking oil

750 ml lukewarm water

50 ml cold water

50 ml poppy, sesame or mixed seeds

Preheat the oven to 200 °C.

Coat two baking sheets with cooking spray and set aside.

1   Mix the flour, salt and sugar in a large mixing bowl. Stir in the yeast.

2   Add the oil and lukewarm water, and mix thoroughly to form a soft dough.

3   Knead the dough in the bowl until smooth and pliable.

4   Turn out onto a lightly floured surface and knead for 10 minutes or until the dough is smooth and elastic.

5   Shape into a ball, place into a large bowl and cover with clingfilm. Set aside in a warm place to rise until the dough has doubled in size.

6   Punch the dough down in the bowl to remove any air bubbles.

7   Divide the dough into 12 equal pieces and roll each into a 15 cm 'rope'. Shape each 'rope' into a circle and seal the ends with the cold water.

8   Place the bagels on a lightly floured surface, cover with clingfilm and set aside in a warm place to prove for 20 minutes.

9   Place three bagels at a time into a large, heavy-based saucepan half-filled with boiling water. Boil the bagels for 1 minute.

10  Remove from the boiling water using a slotted spoon, place on the prepared sheets and sprinkle with the seeds.

11  Bake for 25 minutes or until light brown in colour.

12  Remove from the oven and leave to cool on the sheets for 10 minutes. Turn out onto a wire rack to cool.

## Variations

For cinnamon-raisin bagels: Soak 500 ml seedless raisins in boiling water, drain and add to the dough together with 5 ml ground cinnamon during the final kneading stage prior to boiling the bagels.

For that 'New York' touch: Substitute 750 ml clear apple juice for the 750 ml water.

# Brioche

Makes 12

25 g fresh yeast

125 ml warm water

80 g (100 ml) white sugar

750 g cake flour

5 ml salt

5 ml grated lemon rind

250 g butter, softened

6 jumbo eggs

1 jumbo egg, beaten

Preheat the oven to 180 °C.

Coat eight 8 cm and four 10 cm brioche tins with cooking spray, place onto baking sheets and set aside.

1   Crumble the yeast into the water in a food mixer fitted with the dough hook, sprinkle the sugar over and set aside until frothy.

2   Mix in the flour, salt, lemon rind, butter and eggs, and mix to form a soft dough.

3   Cover the bowl with clingfilm and set aside in a warm place to rise until the dough has doubled in size.

4   Make 12 large and 12 small balls from the dough and place the larger balls into the prepared tins.

5   Make an indentation in each large ball and brush with the egg wash.

6   Place a smaller ball of dough on top of each larger ball.

7   Cover with clingfilm and set aside in a warm place to prove.

8   Remove the clingfilm and brush the brioches with the remaining egg wash.

9   Bake for 20–25 minutes or until golden brown in colour.

10  Remove from the oven and leave to cool in the tins for 5 minutes. Turn out onto a wire rack to cool.

If brioche tins are not available, use a jumbo muffin tin.

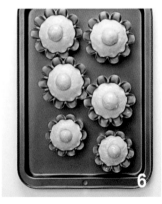

# Earl Grey Tea Glacé Orange Brioche

Makes 12

25 g fresh yeast

1 Earl Grey tea bag steeped in 125 ml hot water

80 g (100 ml) white sugar

750 g cake flour

5 ml salt

5 ml grated lemon rind

250 g butter, softened

6 jumbo eggs

100 g glacé orange, finely chopped

1 jumbo egg, beaten

Preheat the oven to 180 °C.

Coat twelve 8 cm brioche tins with cooking spray, place onto baking sheets and set aside. Crumble the yeast into the tea (from which the tea bag has been removed) in a food mixer fitted with the dough hook, sprinkle the sugar over and set aside until frothy. Mix in the flour, salt, lemon rind, butter and eggs, and mix to form a soft dough. Cover the bowl with clingfilm and set aside in a warm place to rise until the dough has doubled in size.

Remove the clingfilm and add the orange. Make 12 large and 12 small balls from the dough and place the larger balls in the prepared tins. Make an indentation in each large ball and brush with the egg wash. Place a smaller ball of dough on top of each larger ball. Cover with clingfilm and set aside in a warm place to prove. Remove the clingfilm and brush with the remaining egg wash. Bake for 20–25 minutes or until golden brown in colour. Remove from the oven and leave to cool in the tins for 5 minutes. Turn out onto a wire rack to cool. Serve with lashings of butter.

If mini loaf tins are unavailable, use small aluminium foil loaf tins.

# Mini Raisin Breads

Makes 8 mini loaves

500 g cake flour

10 ml salt

5 ml ground cinnamon

25 g fresh yeast

100 ml lukewarm water

80 g (100 ml) white sugar

40 ml butter or margarine

200 ml milk

1 jumbo egg, beaten

150 g (250 ml) seedless raisins

15 ml milk

15 ml white sugar

Preheat the oven to 180 °C.

Coat eight 8 x 5 cm mini loaf tins with cooking spray and set aside. Mix the flour, salt and cinnamon in a large mixing bowl. Crumble the yeast into the water in a small bowl, sprinkle sugar over and set aside until frothy. Heat the butter or margarine and the 200 ml milk in a small bowl in the microwave at 100% power for 2 minutes. Set aside until lukewarm. Add this mixture, the egg and the yeast mixture to the dry ingredients to form a soft dough. Add the raisins. Knead the dough in the bowl until smooth and pliable. Turn the dough out onto a lightly floured surface and knead for 10 minutes or until the dough is smooth and elastic. Shape the dough into a ball, place into a large bowl and cover with clingfilm. Set aside in a warm place to rise until the dough has doubled in size. Turn the dough out onto the lightly floured surface again and punch down to remove any air bubbles. Transfer the dough to the prepared tins and cover with clingfilm. Set aside in a warm place to prove. Remove the clingfilm, brush the tops of the loaves with the 15 ml milk and sprinkle the sugar over. Bake for 25 minutes or until a skewer inserted into the centre comes out clean and the loaves sound hollow when tapped with the knuckles. Remove from the oven and leave to cool in the tins for 5 minutes. Turn out onto a wire rack to cool.

# Fruit Yeast Cake

250 ml milk

25 g fresh yeast

2.5 ml bicarbonate of soda

450 g cake flour

5 ml salt

5 ml mixed spice

100 g butter or margarine

100 g castor sugar

200 g fruit cake mix

2 jumbo eggs, beaten

30 ml honey

Preheat the oven to 180 °C.

Coat a 22 cm round cake tin with cooking spray and set aside.

1   Heat the milk in a small bowl in the microwave at 100% power for 2 minutes. Set aside to cool until lukewarm.

2   Crumble in the yeast. Add the bicarbonate of soda and set aside until frothy.

3   Sift the flour, salt and mixed spice into a large mixing bowl.

4   Rub in the butter or margarine until the mixture resembles breadcrumbs.

5   Stir in the castor sugar and cake mix.

6   Make a well in the centre and mix in the yeast liquid and the eggs. Using a wooden spoon, stir until mixed.

7   Spoon the dough into the prepared tin. Cover with clingfilm and set aside in a warm place to prove.

8   Remove the clingfilm and bake for 45 minutes or until the cake is firm to the touch.

9   Remove from the oven and leave to cool in the tin for 10 minutes. Turn out onto a wire rack to cool.

10  Place the cake on a serving plate and whilst still warm, glaze the top of the cake with the honey.

The cake mixture can also be prepared in a food mixer fitted with the dough hook.

# Danish Pastry

Makes ±30 pastries

800 g cake flour

5 ml salt

25 g fresh yeast

75 ml lukewarm water

75 g white sugar

50 g margarine

350 ml milk

2 jumbo eggs, beaten

5 ml fresh lemon juice

400 g butter, thinly sliced

1 jumbo egg, beaten

**Almond Filling**

50 g butter

50 g icing sugar

30 g ground almonds

1 ml vanilla essence

**Glacé Icing**

25 ml milk

130 g (250 ml) icing sugar, sifted

Preheat the oven to 210 °C.

Coat two baking sheets with cooking spray and set aside.

1   Mix the flour and salt in a large mixing bowl and set aside.

2   Crumble the yeast into the water in a small bowl, sprinkle the sugar over and set aside until frothy.

3   Heat the margarine and milk in a small bowl in the microwave at 100% power for 2 minutes. Set aside to cool until lukewarm.

4   Add the yeast and milk mixtures to the dry ingredients.

5   Stir in the 2 beaten eggs and lemon juice and mix to form a soft dough.

6   Knead the pastry in the bowl until smooth and pliable.

7   Turn the pastry out onto a lightly floured surface and knead for 10 minutes or until the pastry is smooth and elastic.

8   Shape the pastry into a ball, place into a large bowl and cover with clingfilm. Set aside in a warm place until the pastry has doubled in size.

9   Using a palette knife, shape the butter on a sheet of baking paper into a 23 x 7.5 cm rectangle and refrigerate for 10 minutes.

10  Turn the pastry out onto the lightly floured surface again and roll it into a 25 cm square.

11  Place the butter in the centre of the pastry and peel away the baking paper.

12  Fold the unbuttered sides of the pastry over the butter to overlap by 1 cm.

13  Seal the top and bottom ends.

14  Roll the pastry into a 45 x 15 cm rectangle and fold the pastry over evenly into three.

15  Wrap in clingfilm and refrigerate. Repeat the rolling and folding of the pastry twice more, wrap in clingfilm and refrigerate for 10 minutes. The pastry is now ready for filling and shaping.

16  Turn the pastry out onto the lightly floured surface, roll out 5 mm thick and cut into 10 cm squares.

17  Place a teaspoon of almond filling in the centre of the pastry and fold the two opposite corners in to cover the filling.

18  Bake the pastries in batches. Place pastry parcels onto the prepared sheets, brush with the beaten egg, cover with clingfilm and set aside in a warm place to prove.

19  Remove the clingfilm and bake for 20 minutes or until golden brown in colour. Remove from the oven and leave to cool on the sheets for 5 minutes. Turn out onto a wire rack to cool.

**To make the almond filling**

20  Combine the ingredients in a small bowl and refrigerate until ready to use.

**To make the icing**

21  Mix the milk with the icing sugar, a little at a time, until it has the consistency of thin cream.

22  Drizzle the icing over the cooled pastries.

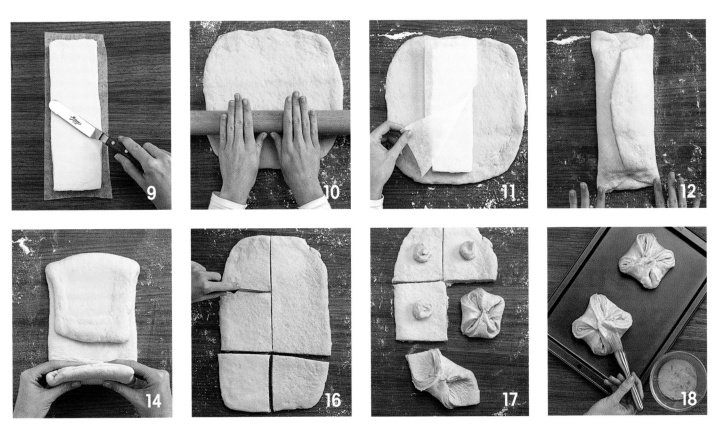

# Chelsea Buns

Makes 12

375 ml warm milk

50 g fresh yeast

10 ml castor sugar

10 ml cake flour

250 ml boiling water

150 g (250 ml) currants

5 ml grated lemon rind

5 ml ground cinnamon

1 kg cake flour

1 jumbo egg, beaten

80 g butter or margarine, melted

160 g (200 ml) golden brown sugar

15 ml castor sugar

1 x quantity Glacé Icing (see Danish Pastry, page 42)

Preheat the oven to 180 °C.

Coat a deep 24 cm square cake tin with cooking spray and set aside. Heat the milk in a bowl in the microwave at 100% power for 2 minutes. Crumble the yeast into the milk, sprinkle the castor sugar and 10 ml flour over, and set aside until frothy. Pour the water over the currants, soak for 10 minutes, then drain. Combine the currants, lemon rind and cinnamon in a small bowl and set aside. Sift the flour into a large mixing bowl. Add the egg and yeast mixture to the flour and mix thoroughly to form a soft dough. Knead the dough in the bowl until smooth and pliable. Shape the dough into a ball, place into a large bowl and cover with clingfilm. Set aside in a warm place to rise until the dough has doubled in size.

Turn the dough out onto a lightly floured surface and roll into a 30 x 40 cm rectangle. Brush with a third of the butter or margarine and sprinkle evenly with one third of the brown sugar. Fold one third of the dough over the middle third and fold the remaining third on top. Seal the ends and turn 90°. Repeat folding as before, using the second third of the butter and sugar. Seal the ends and turn 90°. Repeat folding as before, using the remaining butter and sugar, and sprinkle the currant mixture over. Roll the dough from the long side like a swiss roll, and cut evenly into 12 pieces. Place the buns cut side up into the prepared tin and sprinkle with the castor sugar. Set aside, uncovered, in a warm place to prove. Bake for 25 minutes or until the buns are golden brown in colour. Remove from the oven and turn out onto a wire rack. Drizzle a little icing onto each bun while still warm. Set aside to cool.

Panettone is a traditional, rich Christmas bread that originates from Milan, Italy.

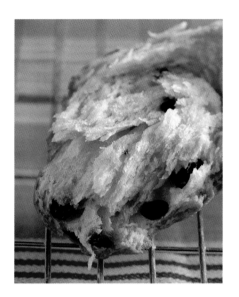

# Marissa's Panettone

Makes 8

| | |
|---|---|
| 250 g fruit cake mix | 125 g white sugar |
| 125 g butter | 400 ml milk |
| 100 ml rum | 150 g butter |
| 800 g cake flour | 25 g fresh yeast |
| 5 ml salt | 2 jumbo eggs |

Preheat the oven to 180 °C.

Coat eight 7 cm diameter panettone paper cases with cooking spray, place on a baking sheet and set aside. Place the cake mix, 125 g butter and rum in a large heavy-based saucepan, and heat until the butter melts. Set aside to cool. Sift the flour, salt and sugar into a bowl. Heat the milk and the 150 g butter in a bowl in the microwave at 100% power for 2 minutes or until the butter has melted. Crumble the yeast into the milk mixture and set aside until frothy. Pour the milk mixture into the flour mixture and mix thoroughly. Add the eggs and knead the dough for 5 minutes. Place the dough in a large bowl and cover with clingfilm. Set aside in a warm place until doubled in size. Knock the dough back, mix in the fruit mixture and knead for 5 minutes. Spoon the dough into the prepared cases and bake for 40–45 minutes or until a skewer inserted into the centre comes out clean. Remove from the oven and leave to cool on the baking sheet for 10 minutes. Turn out onto a wire rack to cool.

**Handy hint:** If panettone paper cases are unavailable, the panettone can be baked in jumbo muffin tins.

# Captivating
# Cakes

*The technique is what makes each cake unique and such a treat.*

# Five Cake-making Methods

## Creaming

Butter or margarine and sugar are beaten together in a food mixer until light and creamy in colour. The eggs are added, followed by the flour and the remaining liquid.

## Whisking

Eggs and sugar are whisked together until light and creamy in colour. The sifted dry ingredients are folded in using a metal spoon and the butter is melted and added. For a lighter sponge, the eggs may be separated and the whites beaten with the sugar to make a meringue. The meringue is folded in with a metal spoon.

## Rubbing-in

The butter or margarine is rubbed into the flour and the raising agent with the fingertips until the mixture resembles breadcrumbs. Alternatively, a food mixer fitted with the plastic blade is used. The eggs are mixed in with the liquid.

## Melting

The butter/margarine, sugar/syrup are heated in a heavy-based saucepan until melted and set aside to cool. The dry ingredients are added, followed by the liquid and eggs.

## Quick-mixing

All the ingredients are combined in a food mixer and spooned into the prepared tin.

# Basic Butter Cake

100 g butter

180 g white sugar

5 ml vanilla essence

2 jumbo eggs

260 g cake flour

10 ml baking powder

1 ml salt

125 ml milk

**Butter Icing**

150 g butter, softened

250 g icing sugar

5 ml vanilla essence

25 ml milk

silver balls, for decorating

Preheat the oven to 180 °C.

Coat a 20 cm round cake tin with cooking spray and set aside.

1  Cream the butter and sugar in the bowl of a food mixer and beat until light and creamy in colour.

2  Add the vanilla essence.

3  Add the eggs one at a time, beating after each addition.

4  Sift the flour, baking powder and salt into a bowl.

5  Add the flour alternately with the milk to the butter mixture.

6  Spoon the batter into the prepared tin and bake for 25 minutes or until a skewer inserted into the centre comes out clean.

7  Remove from the oven and leave to cool in the tin for 15 minutes. Turn out onto a wire rack to cool.

**To make the butter icing**

8  Cream the butter, icing sugar and vanilla essence in a food mixer.

9  Add sufficient milk to make a smooth icing.

**To assemble**

10  When cold, cut the cake in half horizontally and sandwich together with half the icing.

11  Coat the top of the cake with the remaining icing and decorate with the silver balls.

# Delicious Marble Cake

30 ml cocoa powder
50 ml boiling water
250 g butter or margarine
260 g white sugar
400 g cake flour
15 ml baking powder
1 ml salt
4 jumbo eggs
250 ml milk
5 ml vanilla essence
icing sugar, for dusting

Preheat the oven to 180 °C.

Coat a 24 x 11 cm Bundt tin with cooking spray and set aside. Mix the cocoa and boiling water in a small bowl to form a paste and set aside to cool. Cream the butter or margarine and sugar in the bowl of a food mixer until light and creamy in colour. Sift the flour, baking powder and salt into a bowl and set aside. Add the eggs, dry ingredients, milk and vanilla essence to the margarine mixture and beat thoroughly. Divide the mixture into two bowls. Add the cocoa mixture to the one bowl and mix. Spoon the batter into the prepared tin alternating vanilla and chocolate layers. Zigzag through the batter using a palette knife and bake for 1 hour. Remove from the oven and cool in the tin for 15 minutes. Turn out onto a wire rack to cool. Dust with the icing sugar.

**Handy hint:** This recipe makes 12 excellent muffins. Reduce the baking time to 20 minutes.

Un-iced, this cake will keep for up to two days in an airtight container. Hazelnut praline and ganache need to be prepared on the day of serving.

# Chocolate Hazelnut Cake

250 g soft butter, cubed
300 g castor sugar
4 jumbo eggs
150 g ground hazelnuts
300 g self-raising flour, sifted
2.5 ml baking powder
125 ml milk

**Hazelnut Praline**
200 g castor sugar
100 ml water
375 g whole hazelnuts

1 x quantity Ganache (see page 219)

Preheat the oven to 180 °C.

Coat a 22 cm round cake tin with cooking spray. Cream the butter and castor sugar in the bowl of a food mixer until light and creamy in colour. Add the eggs one at a time, beating after each addition. Fold the ground hazelnuts, flour and baking powder alternately with the milk into the butter mixture and mix thoroughly. Spoon into the prepared tin and bake for 55 minutes or until a skewer inserted into the centre comes out clean. Remove from the oven and leave to cool in the tin for 15 minutes. Turn out onto a wire rack to cool.

**To make the hazelnut praline:** Coat a baking sheet with cooking spray and set aside. Heat the castor sugar and water in a small, heavy-based saucepan, and stir until the sugar dissolves. Boil without stirring until golden in colour. Remove from the heat, add the nuts and stir until they are coated in the caramel. Pour the praline onto the prepared baking sheet and set aside to cool. Grind until fine in a food processor fitted with the metal blade.

**To assemble:** Using a serrated knife, cut the cake in half horizontally and sandwich together with half the chocolate ganache. Spread the remaining ganache over the top of the cake and decorate with the hazelnut praline.

**To make the cake on the cover:** Use double the quantity of the cake mixture and spoon into two x 24 cm cake tins. Bake for 55–60 minutes or until a skewer inserted into the centre comes out clean. Ice the cooled cake with chocolate ganache. For the praline, follow the instructions given above but make small clusters instead of pouring the hot praline onto the baking sheet. Allow to cool before decorating the cake.

# Ma's Special Butter Cherry Cake

250 g glacé cherries
25 ml cake flour
250 g butter
250 g castor sugar
4 jumbo eggs
250 g cake flour
5 ml baking powder
2.5 ml salt
5 ml grated lemon rind
15 ml brandy
25 ml milk
15 ml fresh lemon juice
icing sugar, for dusting

Preheat the oven to 170 °C.

Coat a 24 x 11 cm Bundt tin with cooking spray and set aside. Coat the cherries in the 25 ml flour in a small bowl and set aside. Cream the butter and castor sugar in the bowl of a food mixer until light and creamy in colour. Add the eggs one at a time, beating well after each addition. Sift the flour, baking powder and salt in a bowl, and add alternately with the lemon rind, brandy, milk and lemon juice to the butter mixture. Fold in the cherries. Spoon the batter into the prepared tin and bake for 50 minutes. Reduce the oven temperature to 160 °C and bake for a further 10 minutes. Remove from the oven and leave to cool in the tin for 15 minutes. Turn out onto a wire rack to cool. Dust with the icing sugar.

# Peach Cake

3 yellow cling peaches, peeled, halved, stoned
    and cut into wedges or 2 x 410 g cans
    yellow peach slices, drained
125 g butter or margarine
170 g (200 ml) castor sugar
5 ml vanilla essence
4 jumbo eggs
300 g self-raising flour, sifted
100 g (250 ml) ground almonds
125 ml sweet white dessert wine
30 ml golden brown sugar

Preheat the oven to 180 °C.

**For the fresh peaches only:** Stand the peach wedges on a wire rack over a baking sheet and bake for 20 minutes. Set aside to cool.

Coat a 24 cm round springform tin with cooking spray and set aside. Cream the butter or margarine and castor sugar in the bowl of a food mixer until light and creamy in colour. Add the vanilla essence. Add the eggs one at a time, beating thoroughly after each addition. Add the flour and almonds alternately with the wine to the margarine mixture and mix thoroughly. Spoon the batter into the prepared tin and level the top. Arrange fresh peach wedges or canned peach slices in concentric circles over the batter. Sprinkle with the sugar and bake for 50 minutes or until a skewer inserted into the centre comes out clean. Remove from the oven and leave to cool in the tin for 10 minutes. Turn out onto a wire rack to cool.

**Handy hint:** This cake will keep in an airtight container for up to three days and makes a delicious dessert too!

# Basic Sponge Cake

4 jumbo eggs

100 g castor sugar

215 g cake flour

50 ml cornflour

20 ml baking powder

2.5 ml salt

250 ml milk

30 ml butter

2.5 ml vanilla essence

150 ml strawberry jam, warmed

icing sugar, for dusting

fresh strawberries, for decorating

Preheat the oven to 180 °C.

Coat two 21 cm heart-shaped cake tins with cooking spray and set aside.

1 Beat the eggs in a food mixer until thick and foamy.

2 Add the castor sugar 15 ml at a time, beating after each addition.

3 Sift the flour, cornflour, baking powder and salt three times into mixing bowls.

4 Add the flour mixture to the egg mixture 15 ml at a time, mixing thoroughly.

5 Scrape the sides of the bowl from time to time using a spatula.

6 Heat the milk and butter in a small, heavy-based saucepan and bring to the boil. Remove from the heat.

7 With the mixer running, pour the milk and butter mixture down the sides of the bowl. Beat for 1 minute, then add the vanilla essence.

8 Spoon the batter into the prepared tins and bake for 20 minutes or until a skewer inserted into the centre comes out clean.

9 Remove from the oven and turn out onto a wire rack to cool.

**To assemble**

10 Spread the cakes with the jam and sandwich together.

11 Dust with the icing sugar and decorate with fresh strawberries.

This sponge is best eaten on the day it is baked and won't keep, as it only contains a small amount of butter.

# Swiss Roll with Granadilla Filling

4 jumbo eggs, separated

125 g castor sugar

125 g self-raising flour

30 ml milk, heated

25 ml castor sugar

**Granadilla Cream**

250 ml fresh cream, whipped

25 ml lemon curd

8 fresh granadillas, strained

     or 1 x 110 g can granadilla pulp

icing sugar, for dusting

## Passionfruit can be substituted for the granadilla.

Preheat the oven to 180 °C.

Line the base of a 38 x 26 cm swiss roll tin with baking paper. Coat the paper and sides of the tin with cooking spray and set aside.

1  Whisk the egg whites in the bowl of a food mixer until stiff peaks begin to form.

2  Add the castor sugar, 15 ml at a time, beating well after each addition.

3  With the mixer running, add the egg yolks and whisk until the mixture is light and creamy in colour.

4  Sift the flour into a bowl.

5  Add the flour alternately with the milk to the egg mixture.

6  Spoon the batter into the prepared tin and bake for 8 minutes.

### To make the granadilla cream

7  Combine the ingredients in a small bowl and refrigerate until ready to use.

### To assemble

8  Cut a piece of baking paper slightly larger than the swiss roll tin.

9  Place the paper on a tea towel and sprinkle with the 25 ml castor sugar.

10  Invert the baked swiss roll onto the sugared paper.

11  Peel away the paper lining and cut away 5 mm from all the edges of the swiss roll. This removes the crisp edges and makes rolling easier.

12  Using a palette knife, make a shallow cut halfway into the swiss roll, 2.5 cm from and parallel to the end to be rolled.

13  Without filling it, press the cut end over and hold down with one hand.

14  Grip the paper with the other hand. Working away from you, roll up the swiss roll. Hold the paper around the roll for a few seconds.

15  Unroll and allow to cool.

16  Spread the filling over the swiss roll to within 2.5 cm of the end.

17  Roll into shape again.

18  Dust with the icing sugar.

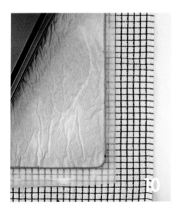

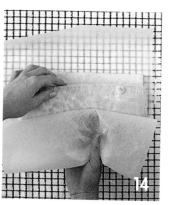

# Chocolate Brandy Roll

120 g cake flour

50 ml cocoa powder

5 ml baking powder

1 ml salt

3 jumbo eggs

200 g (250 ml) white sugar

50 ml water

25 ml brandy

5 ml vanilla essence

**Brandy Cream**

250 ml fresh cream

25 ml brandy

50 ml icing sugar

icing sugar, for dusting

Preheat the oven to 190 °C.

Line the base of a 38 x 26 cm swiss roll tin with baking paper. Coat the paper and tin with cooking spray and set aside. Sift the flour, cocoa, baking powder and salt into a bowl and set aside. Beat the eggs in the bowl of a food mixer until light and creamy in colour. Beat in the sugar, 15 ml at a time, beating thoroughly after each addition. Add the water, brandy and vanilla essence, and beat thoroughly. Fold in the flour mixture using a metal spoon. Spoon the batter into the prepared tin and bake for 10–12 minutes or until a skewer inserted into the centre comes out clean.

**To make the brandy cream:** Beat the cream until stiff in a small mixing bowl. Add the brandy and icing sugar. Refrigerate until ready to use.

**To assemble:** See Step-by-Step Swiss Roll with Granadilla Filling (page 60).

# Genoise Sponge Cake with American Frosting

Makes 2

4 jumbo eggs

100 ml boiling water

170 g (200 ml) castor sugar

75 g cake flour

110 g (200 ml) self-raising flour

1 x quantity American Frosting (see page 219)

sugared cake decorations, for decorating

Preheat the oven to 190 °C.

Line the base of two 23 cm Bundt tins with baking paper. Coat the tins with cooking spray and set aside. Beat the eggs in the bowl of a food mixer for 3–4 minutes. Add the water and beat until the mixture is light and creamy in colour. Add the castor sugar 15 ml at a time, beating after each addition. Sift the flours twice into two mixing bowls and fold into the egg mixture using a metal spoon. Spoon the batter into the prepared tins and bake for 30 minutes or until a skewer inserted into the centre comes out clean. Leave to cool in the tins for 5 minutes and turn out onto a wire rack to cool. Spread the frosting on the top and sides of the cakes and decorate with sugared cake decorations. Sponge cake is best eaten on the same day.

# Coffee Chocolate Cake

230 g cake flour

60 ml cocoa powder

15 ml baking powder

2.5 ml salt

5 jumbo eggs, separated

300 g (375 ml) white sugar

5 ml vanilla essence

200 ml cooking oil

200 ml lukewarm water

2.5 ml cream of tartar

**Coffee Syrup**

375 ml water

330 g golden brown sugar

30 ml instant coffee granules

5 ml vanilla essence

**Condensed Milk Cream**

125 ml fresh cream, whipped

1 x 185 g can caramelised condensed milk

1 x 32 g flaky milk chocolate

Preheat the oven to 180 °C.

Coat a 23 cm round, ring-shaped tin with cooking spray and set aside. Sift the flour, cocoa, baking powder and salt into a bowl and set aside. Beat the egg yolks and sugar in the bowl of a food mixer until light and creamy in colour. Add the vanilla essence, oil and water, and mix thoroughly. Spoon in the dry ingredients and mix. Beat the egg whites and cream of tartar in a bowl until stiff peaks begin to form. Fold the egg whites into the cake mixture using a metal spoon. Pour into the prepared tin. Bake for 40 minutes or until a skewer inserted into the centre comes out clean. Remove from the oven and leave to cool in the tin.

**To make the coffee syrup:** Combine all the ingredients in a medium-sized, heavy-based saucepan and bring to the boil. Remove from the heat. Spoon the hot syrup over the cake in the tin and set aside for 15 minutes. Invert onto a plate and coat with the condensed milk cream when cold.

**To make the condensed milk cream:** Combine the cream and caramelised condensed milk in a small bowl until mixed. Spread over the cake and top with the flaky chocolate.

# Chiffon Cake

340 g cake flour

15 ml baking powder

5 ml salt

7 jumbo eggs, separated

270 g white sugar

125 ml cooking oil

200 ml water

2.5 ml cream of tartar

10 ml grated lemon or orange rind

icing sugar, for dusting

fresh rose petals, for decorating

Preheat the oven to 160 °C.

Use an ungreased 25 cm diameter chiffon tube tin for this cake.

1  Sift the flour, baking powder and salt into the bowl of a food mixer.

2  Add the egg yolks, sugar, oil and water, and mix.

3  Beat the egg whites and cream of tartar in a mixing bowl until stiff peaks begin to form.

4  Fold the egg whites into the flour mixture using a metal spoon.

5  Add the lemon or orange rind.

6  Pour the batter into the tin and bake for 55 minutes.

7  Remove from the oven, invert the tin over a bottle and leave the cake suspended until cool.

8  Run a sharp knife around the edge of the cake tin.

9  Turn the cake out onto a serving platter.

10  Dust with the icing sugar and decorate with fresh rose petals.

**Handy hint:** 'Suspending' the chiffon cake stops the cake from sinking and retains all the trapped air.

For even air distribution, fold the egg whites into the batter using a metal spoon.

# Lemon-Cinnamon Chiffon Cake

340 g cake flour

300 g castor sugar

2.5 ml bicarbonate of soda

2.5 ml salt

15 ml ground cinnamon

125 ml cooking oil

7 jumbo eggs, separated

3 additional jumbo egg whites

200 ml water

30 ml fresh lemon juice

15 ml grated lemon rind

5 ml cream of tartar

50 ml icing sugar

5 ml ground cinnamon

Preheat the oven to 170 °C.

Sift the flour, castor sugar, bicarbonate of soda, salt and 15 ml cinnamon into the bowl of a food mixer. Make a well in the centre and add the oil, egg yolks, water, lemon juice and rind. Beat thoroughly. Beat the egg whites and cream of tartar in a bowl until stiff peaks begin to form. Fold the egg whites into the flour mixture using a metal spoon. Spoon the batter into an ungreased 25 cm diameter chiffon tube tin. Bake for 55 minutes. Remove from the oven, invert the tin over a bottle and leave the cake suspended until cool. Run a sharp knife around the outer edge of the cake tin and turn the cake out onto a serving platter. Combine the icing sugar and cinnamon in a small bowl and spoon over the top of the cake.

# Orange-glazed Chiffon Cake

6 jumbo eggs, separated

330 g castor sugar

125 ml cooking oil

200 ml water

grated rind of 1 orange

2.5 ml cream of tartar

300 g self-raising flour, sifted


**Orange Glaze**

100 ml fresh orange juice

30 ml fresh lemon juice

350 g icing sugar, sifted


20 ml grated orange rind, for decorating

Preheat the oven to 170 °C.

Whisk the egg yolks and the castor sugar in a food mixer until light and creamy in colour. With the mixer running, add the oil, water and orange rind, and beat thoroughly. Whisk the egg whites and cream of tartar in a mixing bowl until stiff peaks begin to form. Spoon the flour into the egg mixture and, using a metal spoon, fold in the egg whites. Spoon the batter into an ungreased 25 cm diameter tube tin and bake for 45–50 minutes. Remove from the oven, invert the tin over a bottle and leave the cake suspended until cool. Run a sharp knife around the outer edge of the cake tin and turn the cake out onto a serving platter.

**To make the orange glaze:** Combine all the ingredients in a small bowl and mix until the mixture has the consistency of thin cream. Pour the glaze over the top of the cake and decorate with the orange rind. The iced cake will keep in an airtight container for up to four days.

This cake has a chocolate, nutty topping and is the perfect

after-school snack for deserving children!

# Chocolate-Cola Cake

Makes 16 squares

240 g cake flour
180 g white sugar
220 g butter or margarine
50 ml cocoa powder
250 ml carbonated cola drink
150 ml buttermilk
2 jumbo eggs
5 ml vanilla essence
5 ml bicarbonate of soda
16 or 100 g marshmallows, quartered

**Icing**

50 ml butter or margarine
50 ml cocoa powder
75 ml carbonated cola drink
250 g icing sugar
80 g chopped pecan nuts

Preheat the oven to 180 °C.

Coat a 23 cm square cake tin with cooking spray and set aside. Mix the flour and sugar in the bowl of a food mixer fitted with the plastic blade. Heat the butter or margarine, cocoa and cola in a medium-sized, heavy-based saucepan. Stir and bring to the boil, then set aside to cool. Add the buttermilk, eggs, vanilla essence and bicarbonate of soda to the flour mixture. Pour in the margarine mixture and mix in the marshmallows. Spoon the batter into the prepared tin and bake for 35 minutes or until a skewer inserted into the centre comes out clean.

**To make the icing:** Melt the butter or margarine in a small, heavy-based saucepan. Add the cocoa and cola, and bring to the boil. Sift the icing sugar into a mixing bowl and pour in the cola mixture. Stir in the pecan nuts. Spread the icing over the warm cake and set aside to cool. Cut into squares and remove from the tin.

# Pistachio, Yoghurt and Cardamom Cake

150 g (250 ml) unsalted pistachios

5 ml ground cardamom

150 g unsalted butter

200 g self-raising flour

200 g castor sugar

3 jumbo eggs

1 x 175 g tub low-fat plain yoghurt

**Syrup**

rind of 1 lemon, cut into long, thin strips

125 g castor sugar

100 ml water

**Frosting**

250 ml milk

250 ml thin fresh cream

5 jumbo egg yolks

100 g castor sugar

2.5 ml vanilla essence

Preheat the oven to 180 °C.

Coat a 21 x 11 cm Bundt tin with cooking spray and set aside. Coarsely chop the pistachios and cardamom in a food mixer fitted with the metal blade. Replace the metal blade with the plastic blade. Add the butter, flour and castor sugar, and mix until the mixture resembles breadcrumbs. Add the eggs and yoghurt, and mix thoroughly. Spoon the batter into the prepared tin and bake for 40–45 minutes or until a skewer inserted into the centre comes out clean. Remove from the oven and leave to cool in the tin for 10 minutes. Turn out onto a wire rack to cool.

**To make the syrup:** Place the castor sugar and water in a small, heavy-based saucepan and stir until the sugar dissolves. Bring to the boil. Add the lemon rind and boil for 5 minutes. Remove the rind and set aside the syrup to cool. Place the cake on a serving plate, pierce the top with a skewer and pour the syrup over the cooled cake.

**To make the frosting:** Heat the milk and cream in a small, heavy-based saucepan and bring to the boil. Remove from the heat. Mix the egg yolks, castor sugar and vanilla essence in a bowl and beat until light and creamy in colour. Add the milk mixture to the egg mixture and stir to combine. Pour the mixture back into the saucepan and heat, stirring continuously with a wooden spoon, until the mixture thickens enough to coat the back of the spoon. Do not boil or the mixture will curdle. Remove from the heat. Serve slices of cake drizzled with the frosting.

# Dark Chocolate Carrot Cake

185 g butter

10 ml grated orange rind

160 g castor sugar

2 jumbo eggs

15 ml golden syrup

375 ml coarsely grated carrots

200 g self-raising flour, sifted

2.5 ml bicarbonate of soda

75 ml cocoa powder

200 ml milk

1 x quantity Cream Cheese Icing
   (see page 212)

Preheat the oven to 175 °C.

Coat a 21 x 11 cm Bundt tin with cooking spray and set aside. Cream the butter, orange rind and castor sugar in the bowl of a food mixer fitted with the plastic blade. Beat in the eggs and syrup, and transfer to a large mixing bowl. Stir in the carrots, flour, bicarbonate of soda, cocoa and milk. Spoon the batter into the prepared tin and bake for 40 minutes or until a skewer inserted into the centre comes out clean. Remove from the oven and leave to cool in the tin for 10 minutes. Turn out onto a wire rack to cool. Coat with the cream cheese icing.

# Orange Cake with Granadilla Icing

150 g butter

165 g castor sugar

15 ml grated orange rind

2 jumbo eggs

200 g self-raising flour, sifted

100 ml fresh orange juice

**Granadilla Icing**

260 g (500 ml) icing sugar, sifted

15 ml butter

pulp from 1 large granadilla
   or 30 ml canned pulp

30 ml milk

Preheat the oven to 180 °C.

Coat a 21 x 11 cm Bundt tin with cooking spray and set aside. Cream the butter, castor sugar and rind in the bowl of a food mixer fitted with the plastic blade until light and creamy in colour. Add the eggs one at a time, beating well after each addition. Add the flour alternately with the orange juice to the butter mixture and mix thoroughly. Spoon the batter into the prepared tin and bake for 30 minutes or until a skewer inserted into the centre comes out clean. Remove from the oven and leave to cool in the tin for 10 minutes. Turn out onto a wire rack to cool.

**To make the icing:** Heat the icing sugar, butter and pulp in a double boiler over simmering water. Add the milk and stir until smooth. Remove from the heat and pour over the cooled cake. Iced, the cake will keep in an airtight container for up to three days.

**Note:** Passionfruit can be substituted for the granadilla.

# Date and Pecan Nut Loaf

125 g butter or margarine

110 g castor sugar

200 g pitted dates, chopped

200 ml milk

15 ml golden syrup

260 g self-raising flour, sifted

2 jumbo eggs

60 g pecan nuts, chopped

Preheat the oven to 180 °C.

1   Line the base of a 35 x 13 cm loaf tin with baking paper. Coat the tin with cooking spray and set aside.

2   Heat the butter or margarine, castor sugar, dates, milk and syrup in a large, heavy-based saucepan.

3   Stir until the butter melts and the sugar dissolves.

4   Place the lid on the saucepan and simmer for 2–3 minutes.

5   Remove the saucepan from the heat and stir in the flour, eggs and nuts. Mix thoroughly.

6   Spoon the batter into the prepared tin and bake for 50 minutes or until a skewer inserted into the centre comes out clean.

7   Remove from the oven and leave to cool in the tin for 10 minutes.

8   Turn out onto a wire rack to cool.

9   Serve sliced, spread liberally with butter or cream cheese. The loaf will keep in an airtight container for up to three days.

# Chocolate Date Loaf

5 ml bicarbonate of soda

250 ml boiling water

180 g pitted dates, chopped

90 g butter or margarine

200 g castor sugar

2 jumbo eggs

270 g cake flour

7.5 ml baking powder

5 ml ground cinnamon

1 ml salt

45 ml cocoa powder

Preheat the oven to 180 °C.

Coat a 33 x 13 cm loaf tin with cooking spray and set aside. Combine the bicarbonate of soda, water and dates in a small bowl, and set aside to cool. Cream the butter or margarine and castor sugar in the bowl of a food mixer until light and creamy in colour. Add the eggs one at a time, beating thoroughly after each addition. Sift the flour, baking powder, cinnamon, salt and the cocoa into a bowl. Add alternately with the date mixture to the butter mixture. Spoon the batter into the prepared tin and bake for 55–60 minutes or until a skewer inserted into the centre comes out clean. Remove from the oven and leave to cool in the tin for 10 minutes, then turn out onto a wire rack.

# Banana-Nut Loaf

230 g cake flour

10 ml baking powder

2.5 ml bicarbonate of soda

1 ml salt

80 g butter or margarine

160 g (200 ml) golden brown sugar

2 jumbo eggs

250 ml mashed ripe banana

60 g chopped walnuts

Preheat the oven to 180 °C.

Coat a 25 x 14 cm loaf tin with cooking spray and set aside. Sift the flour, baking powder, bicarbonate of soda and salt into a bowl. Cream the butter or margarine and sugar in the bowl of a food mixer fitted with the plastic blade until light and creamy in colour. Add the eggs one at a time, beating thoroughly after each addition. Spoon the dry ingredients alternately with the banana and nuts into the margarine mixture, and mix. Spoon the batter into the prepared tin and bake for 45 minutes or until a skewer inserted into the centre comes out clean. Remove from the oven and leave to cool in the tin for 10 minutes. Turn out onto a wire rack to cool. Leave in a sealed container overnight before slicing. Serve sliced with butter on the side.

# One-bowl Orange Loaf Cake

280 g (500 ml) cake flour

170 g castor sugar

10 ml baking powder

1 ml salt

125 ml cooking oil

125 ml fresh orange juice

5 ml grated orange rind

2 jumbo eggs

2.5 ml vanilla essence

**Orange Glaze**

10 ml butter or margarine

50 ml fresh orange juice

130 g (250 ml) icing sugar, sifted

Preheat the oven to 160 °C.

Coat a 25 x 14 cm loaf tin with cooking spray and set aside. Sift the flour, castor sugar, baking powder and salt into the bowl of a food mixer fitted with the plastic blade. Add the oil, orange juice and rind, and mix thoroughly. Beat in the eggs and vanilla essence, and spoon the batter into the prepared tin. Bake for 50–55 minutes or until a skewer inserted into the centre comes out clean. Remove from the oven and leave to cool in the tin for 5 minutes. Turn out onto a wire rack to cool.

**To make the orange glaze:** Heat the butter or margarine and juice in a small, heavy-based saucepan, add the icing sugar and stir until smooth. Remove from the heat and set aside to cool slightly. Pour the glaze over the top of the cake, allowing it to trickle down the sides.

# Marmalade-Yoghurt Loaf

225 g cake flour

10 ml baking powder

220 g castor sugar

3 jumbo eggs

250 ml Greek-style, plain yoghurt

grated rind of 1 orange

5 ml vanilla essence

125 ml cooking oil

75 ml good-quality orange marmalade, warmed

extra marmalade, for serving

Preheat the oven to 175 °C.

Coat a 33 x 13 cm loaf tin with cooking spray and set aside. Sift the flour and baking powder into the bowl of a food mixer. Add the remaining ingredients, except the marmalade, and beat on high speed for 1–2 minutes. Spoon the batter into the prepared tin and bake for 55 minutes or until a skewer inserted into the centre comes out clean. Remove from the oven and leave to cool in the tin for 5 minutes. Turn out onto a wire rack to cool, with a plate underneath. Prick the top of the loaf with a skewer and pour over the warmed marmalade. Serve sliced into fingers with extra marmalade on the side.

# Eggless Orange Olive Oil Cake
Makes 6 mini cakes

225 g self-raising flour, sifted

50 g (60 ml) castor sugar

250 ml milk

200 ml olive oil

30 ml grated orange rind

45 ml fresh orange juice

5 ml vanilla essence

2.5 ml almond essence

icing sugar, for dusting

Preheat the oven to 180 °C.

Coat six 10 cm mini Bundt tins with cooking spray and set aside. Combine the flour and castor sugar in a large mixing bowl. Make a well in the centre, stir in the milk and olive oil, and mix thoroughly. Add the rind, orange juice, vanilla and almond essence. Spoon the batter into the prepared tins and bake for 20 minutes or until a skewer inserted into the centre comes out clean. Remove from the oven and leave to cool in the tins for 10 minutes. Turn out onto a wire rack to cool. Dust with the icing sugar. The cakes will keep in an airtight container for 4–5 days.

# Orange Peel Loaf

1 large orange, unpeeled, halved
    and pips removed
100 g sultanas
50 g pecan nuts, chopped
180 g cake flour, sifted
1 ml salt
5 ml bicarbonate of soda
250 g white sugar
125 g butter or margarine
3 jumbo eggs
250 ml milk

**Topping**
45 ml white sugar
5 ml ground cinnamon

Preheat the oven to 180 °C.

Coat a 25 x 14 cm loaf tin with cooking spray and set aside. Chop the orange finely in the bowl of a food mixer fitted with the metal blade. Mix in the sultanas and nuts, then spoon into a small bowl and set aside. Replace the metal blade with the plastic blade. Add the flour, salt and bicarbonate of soda to the bowl and mix. Add the sugar, butter or margarine, eggs and milk, and mix. Stir in the fruit and nut mixture, and spoon the batter into the prepared tin. Bake for 40 minutes or until a skewer inserted into the centre comes out clean. Remove from the oven and leave to cool in the tin for 10 minutes. Turn out onto a wire rack to cool.

**To make the topping:** Combine the sugar and cinnamon in a small bowl and sprinkle over the top of the baked loaf.

# Apple Cake

200 g cake flour

10 ml baking powder

5 ml salt

360 g white sugar

5 ml ground cinnamon

250 ml cooking oil

125 ml milk

3 jumbo eggs

5 ml vanilla essence

3 Granny Smith apples, peeled, cored and diced

100 g (250 ml) chopped walnuts

75 g (125 ml) seedless raisins

30 ml icing sugar, for dusting

Preheat the oven to 180 °C.

Coat a 23 cm Bundt tin with cooking spray and set aside. Sift the flour, baking powder and salt into the bowl of a food mixer. Mix in the sugar, cinnamon, oil, milk, eggs and vanilla essence. Beat thoroughly for 2 minutes. Stir in the apples, nuts and raisins. Spoon the batter into the prepared tin and bake for 70 minutes or until a skewer inserted into the centre comes out clean. Remove from the oven and leave to cool in the tin for 10 minutes. Turn out onto a wire rack to cool. Decorate with baby apples and dust with icing sugar.

# American Cheesecake

Makes 4

160 g (200 ml) white sugar
280 g (500 ml) self-raising flour
120 g butter
1 jumbo egg, beaten

**Filling**
3 x 250 g tubs smooth cream cheese
100 g castor sugar
250 ml fresh cream
4 jumbo eggs
5 ml vanilla essence
15 ml grated lemon rind
100 ml fresh lemon juice

Preheat the oven to 160 °C.

Coat four 10 cm round springform tins with cooking spray and set aside. Combine the sugar and flour in a bowl and rub in the butter. Add the egg and mix into a pliable dough. Press into the prepared tins and place in the fridge until ready to use.

**To make the filling:** Beat the cream cheese, castor sugar, cream and eggs in a food mixer until smooth. Beat in the vanilla essence, lemon rind and juice. Pour the mixture into the prepared bases and bake for 30 minutes. Reduce the oven temperature to 140 °C and bake for a further 30 minutes. Switch off the oven and, without opening the door, leave the cheesecakes in the oven for 30 minutes before removing and allowing to cool. Decorate with fresh cherries.

# Lemon Cheesecake with Berry Compote

1 x 250 g packet digestive biscuits

30 ml golden brown sugar

100 g unsalted butter

**Filling**

2 x 250 g tubs smooth cream cheese

200 g castor sugar

3 jumbo eggs

30 ml cornflour

250 ml sour cream

grated rind and juice of 1 lemon

**Berry Compote**

250 g fresh or frozen raspberries

60 g castor sugar

15 ml grated orange rind

350 g mixed fresh or frozen summer
    berries (halved small strawberries,
    raspberries and blueberries)

30 ml icing sugar, for dusting

Preheat the oven to 160 °C.

Line the base of a 23 cm round springform tin with baking paper, coat the tin with cooking spray and set aside. Crush the biscuits finely in a food mixer fitted with the metal blade and spoon into a small mixing bowl, add the brown sugar and set aside. Melt the butter in a small bowl in the microwave at 100% power for 1½ minutes and combine with the crumbs. Press the crumb mixture onto the base of the prepared tin. Refrigerate until firm.

**To make the filling:** Beat the cream cheese, castor sugar and eggs in a food mixer until smooth. Add the cornflour, sour cream, lemon rind and juice, and beat thoroughly. Pour the filling onto the prepared base and bake for 1 hour until just set, but slightly wobbly in the centre. Switch off the oven and, without opening the door, leave the cheesecake in the oven for 2 hours.

**To make the berry compote:** Combine the raspberries, castor sugar and orange rind in a bowl, and crush with the back of a fork to purée. Stir in the mixed berries. Pour into a bowl and chill until ready to serve.

**To serve:** Remove the cake from the tin and transfer to a serving plate. Dust with the icing sugar. Cut into wedges and serve topped with the berry compote.

# Glacé Orange Cheesecake

1 x 250 g packet digestive biscuits

100 g walnuts, chopped

120 g (200 ml) glacé orange, finely chopped

glacé orange slices, for decorating


**Filling**

1 x 250 g tub mascarpone cheese

300 g ricotta cheese, drained

1 x 250 g tub smooth cream cheese

5 ml vanilla essence

150 g castor sugar

4 jumbo eggs

60 ml fresh lemon juice

grated rind of 1 orange

grated rind of 1 lemon

250 ml fresh cream


icing sugar, for dusting

Preheat the oven to 160 °C.

Coat a 23 cm round springform tin with cooking spray and set aside. Crush the biscuits finely in a food mixer fitted with the metal blade and spoon into a small mixing bowl. Add the walnuts. Press two-thirds of the crumb mixture onto the base of the tin and place in the freezer for 10 minutes. Remove from the freezer and sprinkle the glacé orange over.

**To make the filling:** Mix the mascarpone, ricotta and cream cheese in the bowl of a food mixer and beat thoroughly. Add the vanilla essence, castor sugar and eggs, and mix until smooth. Add the lemon juice, rinds and cream, and mix thoroughly. Pour the filling onto the prepared base and bake for 1 hour until just set, but slightly wobbly in the centre. Switch off the oven and, without opening the door, leave the cheesecake in the oven for 30 minutes. Remove from the oven, top with the remaining crumbs and refrigerate. When ready to serve, decorate with glacé oranges and dust with icing sugar.

# Blueberry Cheesecake

1 x 225 g packet sweet wholewheat biscuits
100 g oats
30 ml caramel brown sugar
50 g butter

**Filling**

2 x 250 g tubs smooth cream cheese
100 g castor sugar
1 x 250 g tub crème fraîche
1 x 250 g tub mascarpone cheese
4 jumbo eggs
25 ml cake flour

**Topping**

250 g fresh or frozen blueberries, defrosted
100 ml blackberry jam
60 ml cherry brandy, or brandy

Preheat the oven to 180 °C.

Line the base of a 30 x 11 cm springform tin with baking paper. Coat the tin with cooking spray and set aside. Crush the biscuits finely in the bowl of a food mixer fitted with the metal blade and spoon into a small mixing bowl. Add the oats and brown sugar, and set aside. Melt the butter in a small bowl in the microwave at 100% power for 1½ minutes and combine with the crumbs. Press the crumb mixture onto the base of the prepared tin. Place in the freezer for 15 minutes until firm.

**To make the filling:** Beat the cream cheese, castor sugar, crème fraîche and mascarpone in the bowl of a food mixer until smooth. Beat in the eggs and flour. Remove the tin from the freezer and place on a baking sheet. Pour the filling into the prepared base. Bake for 45 minutes until just set, but slightly wobbly in the centre. Switch off the oven and, without opening the door, leave the cheesecake in the oven for 30 minutes. Remove the cheesecake from the oven and leave to cool to room temperature.

**To make the topping:** Scatter the blueberries over the cheesecake. Warm the jam and brandy in a small, heavy-based saucepan. Remove from the heat and set aside to cool slightly. Brush the jam mixture over the blueberries, then refrigerate the cheesecake for several hours or overnight until thoroughly chilled.

# *Tantalising* Tea Cakes

*Special cakes for special occasions.*

# Celebrate with Cakes

Cakes are made to celebrate almost any event you can think of. They can be as simple as a square sandwiched together with apricot preserve and topped with a sprinkling of icing sugar or a multi-tiered affair with a rich filling and icing.

Cake making requires precision and careful attention to detail. A slight mismeasurement of ingredients or the failure to follow a specific mixing instruction can drastically alter the flavour and texture of the cake.

The correct oven temperature cannot be stressed enough – check your oven temperature with an oven thermometer from time to time.

Baking tins need sufficient space in the oven. Cakes placed too close together will rise toward each other and end up being lopsided. Cakes placed too close to the oven walls won't rise as high on the side nearest the wall.

# Austrian Coffee Cake

360 g butter

360 g castor sugar

6 jumbo eggs

360 g self-raising flour, sifted

2.5 ml salt

7.5 ml vanilla essence

100 ml water

**Syrup**

5 ml strong instant coffee granules

25 ml white sugar

200 ml boiling water

50 ml brandy

Preheat the oven to 180 °C.

Coat a 22 x 7 cm Bundt tin with cooking spray and set aside. Cream the butter and castor sugar in a food mixer until light and creamy in colour. Beat in the eggs. Mix in the flour and salt. Stir in the vanilla essence and water, and spoon the batter into the prepared tin. Bake for 45 minutes or until a skewer inserted into the centre comes out clean. Remove from the oven and turn out onto a wire rack with a plate underneath. Prick the top of the cake with a skewer and pour the cooled syrup over the hot cake.

**To make the syrup:** Dissolve the coffee and sugar in the boiling water in a small bowl and add the brandy. Set aside until cool.

# Hot Tea Cakes
Makes 4

50 ml sugar

2 jumbo eggs

140 g (250 ml) cake flour

10 ml baking powder

2.5 ml salt

125 ml milk

50 g butter

**Syrup**

100 g butter

100 ml golden syrup or 5 ml Marmite
    yeast extract

Preheat the oven to 180 °C.

Coat four 10 cm mini Bundt tins with cooking spray and set aside. Beat the sugar and eggs in a food mixer until light and creamy in colour. Sift the dry ingredients into a bowl and set aside. Heat the milk and butter in the microwave at 100% power for 1½ minutes or until melted. Add the dry ingredients alternately with the milk mixture to the sugar mixture, and mix. Spoon the batter into the prepared tins and bake for 25 minutes or until a skewer inserted into the centre comes out clean. Prick the tops of the cakes with a skewer and pour the hot syrup over each one. Remove from the tins.

**To make the syrup:** Heat the butter and syrup or Marmite in a small heavy-based saucepan and bring to the boil. Remove from the heat and pour over the hot cakes.

# Chocolate-Yoghurt Cake

110 g butter or margarine

200 g (250 ml) white sugar

3 jumbo eggs

300 g cake flour

7.5 ml baking powder

2.5 ml bicarbonate of soda

100 ml milk

1 x 175 g tub low-fat plain yoghurt

10 ml vanilla essence

**Chocolate Syrup**

150 g butter or margarine

250 ml milk

160 g (200 ml) white sugar

75 ml cocoa powder

whipped cream, for serving

Preheat the oven to 190 °C.

Coat a 25 cm square ceramic dish with cooking spray and set aside. Cream the butter or margarine and sugar in a food mixer. Add the eggs one at a time, beating thoroughly after each addition. Sift the dry ingredients into a bowl and add alternately with the milk and the yoghurt to the margarine mixture. Mix in the vanilla essence. Spoon the batter into the prepared dish and bake for 35 minutes or until a skewer inserted into the centre comes out clean. Remove from the oven. Prick the top of the cake with a skewer and pour the chocolate syrup over the cake. Serve with whipped cream on the side.

**To make the chocolate syrup:** Place all the ingredients in a small, heavy-based saucepan and bring to the boil. Remove from the heat and set aside to cool.

# Pecan Coffee Cake with Maple Syrup Topping

**Maple Syrup Topping**

60 g unsalted butter

75 ml maple syrup

110 g golden brown sugar

100 g (250 ml) whole pecan nuts

120 g unsalted butter

210 g (250 ml) castor sugar

5 ml vanilla essence

60 g chopped pecan nuts or walnuts

2 jumbo eggs, separated

200 g cake flour

10 ml baking powder

2.5 ml salt

125 ml milk

15 ml strong instant coffee granules

**To make the topping:** Coat a 23 cm round cake tin with cooking spray and set aside. Place the butter, syrup and sugar in a small, heavy-based saucepan and bring to the boil. Remove from the heat and pour the mixture into the prepared tin. Arrange the pecan nuts, rounded side down, in concentric circles in the topping mixture.

Preheat the oven to 180 °C.

Cream the butter and castor sugar in a food mixer until light and creamy in colour. Mix in the vanilla essence, nuts and egg yolks. Sift the flour, baking powder and salt into a bowl. Add the flour mixture and the milk alternately to the egg mixture. Mix in the coffee. Whisk the egg whites in a bowl until stiff peaks begin to form and fold into the batter using a metal spoon. Spoon the batter onto the prepared topping and bake for 50 minutes or until the cake pulls away from the sides of the tin and a skewer inserted into the centre comes out clean. Remove from the oven and leave to cool in the tin for 20 minutes. Run a sharp knife around the edge of the tin and invert the cake onto a serving plate.

# Glacé Fruit Loaves

Makes 2 loaves

340 g whole brazil nuts

100 g (250 ml) whole pecan nuts

200 g red glacé cherries

100 g green glacé cherries

1 kg mixed glacé fruit, such as ginger,
    pineapple, orange, watermelon and
    apricot, coarsely chopped

150 g cake flour, sifted

5 ml mixed spice

110 g castor sugar

4 jumbo eggs, beaten

50 ml brandy

Preheat the oven to 150 °C.

Coat two 21 x 7 cm loaf tins with cooking spray and set aside. Combine the nuts and fruit in a large mixing bowl. Coat the fruit with the flour and mixed spice. Whisk the castor sugar, eggs and brandy in a food mixer until light and creamy in colour. Pour into the fruit mixture and mix until thoroughly combined. Spoon the mixture into the tins and bake for 1½ hours or until light brown in colour. Remove from the oven and leave to cool completely in the tins. Turn out onto a wire rack. Serve cut into slices with cups and cups of hot tea! Fruit loaves will keep, wrapped in clingfilm and stored in a cool place, for up to 2 weeks.

# Lemon Syrup Cake

250 g butter or margarine
15 ml grated lemon rind
220 g castor sugar
3 jumbo eggs
45 g desiccated coconut
30 g ground almonds
30 ml fresh lemon juice
250 g self-raising flour, sifted
200 ml low-fat plain yoghurt

**Lemon Syrup**
juice and rind of 1 lemon
125 ml water
75 ml honey
2.5 ml ground ginger

fresh roses, for decorating

Preheat the oven to 190 °C.

Coat a 21 x 11 cm Bundt tin with cooking spray and set aside. Cream the butter or margarine, rind and castor sugar in a food mixer until light and creamy in colour. Add the eggs one at a time, beating thoroughly after each addition. Mix in the coconut, almonds, lemon juice, flour and yoghurt. Spoon the batter into the prepared tin and bake for 45 minutes or until a skewer inserted into the centre comes out clean. Remove from the oven and leave to cool in the tin for 5 minutes. Turn out onto a wire rack with a plate underneath. Prick the top of the cake with a skewer and pour the hot syrup over the hot cake. Decorate with fresh roses.

**To make the syrup:** Heat all the ingredients in a small, heavy-based saucepan, stirring until the honey melts. Bring to the boil, reduce the heat and simmer for 5 minutes. Pour over the cake.

# Flourless Almond Cake with Orange Syrup

2 medium oranges, whole and unpeeled

240 g whole almonds

210 g (250 ml) castor sugar

6 jumbo eggs

5 ml baking powder

5 ml vanilla essence

**Orange Syrup**

100 g castor sugar

75 ml fresh orange juice

75 ml water

icing sugar, for dusting

Preheat the oven to 180 °C.

Line the base of a 24 cm round springform tin with baking paper. Coat the tin with cooking spray and set aside. Place the whole oranges in a medium-sized, heavy-based saucepan in sufficient hot water to cover. Cover the saucepan and bring to the boil. Simmer for 2 hours or until the oranges are tender, replenishing with boiling water if necessary. Drain the oranges and set aside to cool. Quarter the oranges, remove the pips, then chop coarsely in a food mixer and set aside.

Grind the almonds and castor sugar in a food mixer fitted with the metal blade. Transfer the mixture to a bowl and set aside. Replace the metal blade with the plastic blade. Beat the eggs and mix in the baking powder and vanilla essence. Spoon in the almond mixture and the oranges, and mix. Spoon the batter into the prepared tin and bake for 40 minutes or until a skewer inserted into the centre comes out clean. Remove from the oven and leave to cool in the tin for 30 minutes. Turn out onto a wire rack with a plate underneath. Prick the top of the cake with a skewer and pour the hot syrup over. When cool, dust with icing sugar.

**To make the orange syrup:** Place the castor sugar, orange juice and water in a small, heavy-based saucepan and bring to the boil. Simmer for 5 minutes or until slightly thickened.

# Yoghurt Cake with Orange Spice Syrup

4 jumbo eggs, separated

100 g castor sugar

100 ml honey

300 g cake flour

15 ml baking powder

1 ml salt

100 g butter or margarine, melted

15 ml grated orange rind

500 ml Greek-style, plain yoghurt

**Orange Spice Syrup**

220 g castor sugar

125 ml water

3 cardamom pods, lightly crushed

1 cinnamon stick

15 ml grated orange rind

fresh roses and grated orange rind, for decorating

Preheat the oven to 190 °C.

Coat a 23 cm round cake tin with cooking spray and set aside. Beat the egg yolks, castor sugar and honey in a food mixer until light and creamy in colour. Sift the flour, baking powder and salt into a bowl and add to the egg yolk mixture. Mix in the butter or margarine, rind and yoghurt. Whisk the egg whites in a bowl until stiff peaks begin to form and fold into the batter using a metal spoon. Spoon the batter into the prepared tin and bake for 45 minutes or until a skewer inserted into the centre comes out clean. Prick the top of the cake with a skewer and pour the syrup over the cake. Cool the cake in the tin, then remove. Decorate with roses and grated orange rind. The cake will keep in an airtight container for 3–4 days.

**To make the orange spice syrup:** Place the castor sugar and water in a small, heavy-based saucepan and heat, stirring, until the sugar dissolves. Add the spices and orange rind and bring to the boil. Boil for 5 minutes or until the syrup has thickened slightly. Remove the cinnamon stick before using.

# Ma's Fruitcake

Makes 1 x 3.2 kg cake

500 ml water

500 g seedless raisins

500 g currants

500 g sultanas

500 g (625 ml) white sugar

250 g butter or margarine

250 g mixed citrus peel

250 g (625 ml) whole mixed
   nuts, chopped

250 g dates, pitted and chopped

250 g dried apricots, chopped

250 g glacé cherries

10 ml bicarbonate of soda

1 kg cake flour

2.5 ml salt

10 ml baking powder

4 jumbo eggs, beaten

175 ml brandy

Preheat the oven to 150 °C.

Line a 28 cm square cake tin with a double thickness of greased brown paper, extending the paper 10 cm above the edge of the tin. Place the water, raisins, currants, sultanas, sugar and butter or margarine in a large, heavy-based saucepan, and bring to the boil, stirring continuously. Cover and simmer for 30 minutes. Remove from the heat and add the citrus peel, nuts, dates, apricots and cherries. Return to the heat and boil for 5 minutes. Remove the saucepan from the heat and mix in the bicarbonate of soda. Set aside to cool.

Sift the flour, salt and baking powder into a bowl and set aside. Mix the eggs, 50 ml brandy and the dry ingredients into the fruit mixture. Spoon the batter into the prepared tin and bake for 1 hour. Reduce the oven temperature to 120 °C and bake for a further 2 hours. Remove from the oven and leave to cool in the tin for 15 minutes. Prick the top of the cake with a skewer and pour over the remaining brandy. Wrap immediately in double layers of aluminium foil and keep wrapped until ready to use. The cake will keep, refrigerated, for one month and frozen for up to three months.

# Summer Fruitcake with Orange Mascarpone Cream

250 g unsalted butter

250 g castor sugar

6 jumbo eggs

125 ml sour cream

200 g (500 ml) ground almonds

200 g cake flour

7.5 ml baking powder

5 ml vanilla essence

150 g fresh raspberries

150 g fresh blueberries

1 fresh yellow cling peach, peeled
    and sliced

icing sugar, for dusting


**Orange Mascarpone Cream**

200 g mascarpone cheese

150 ml thick fresh cream

25 ml fresh orange juice

10 ml grated orange rind

Preheat the oven to 180 °C.

Coat a 24 cm round springform tin with cooking spray and set aside. Cream the butter and castor sugar in a food mixer and beat until light and creamy in colour. Add the eggs one at a time, beating thoroughly after each addition. Mix in the sour cream and almonds. Sift the flour and baking powder into a bowl and fold into the egg mixture. Add the vanilla essence.

Spoon half the batter into the prepared tin and sprinkle with half the fruit. Spoon in the remaining batter and top with the remaining fruit. Bake for 1 hour or until a skewer inserted into the centre comes out clean. Remove from the oven and leave to cool in the tin for 15 minutes. Turn out onto a wire rack to cool. Dust with the icing sugar and serve with the orange mascarpone cream on the side.

**To make the orange mascarpone cream:** Combine all the ingredients in a bowl. Cover and refrigerate until ready to use.

# Orange Madeleines
Makes 12

100 g unsalted butter

15 ml honey

5 ml vanilla essence

140 g (250 ml) cake flour

5 ml baking powder

2.5 ml ground cardamom

1 ml salt

80 g white sugar

2 jumbo eggs

**Orange Glaze**

150 g icing sugar

5 ml grated orange rind

30 ml fresh orange juice

Preheat the oven to 160 °C.

Coat the moulds of a madeleine tin with cooking spray and set aside. Heat the butter in a small, heavy-based saucepan until melted. Remove from the heat, stir in the honey and vanilla essence and set aside. Sift the flour, baking powder, cardamom and salt into a bowl and set aside. Whisk the sugar and eggs in a food mixer until light and creamy in colour. Fold the flour and butter mixtures alternately into the sugar mixture. Mix thoroughly. Cover the bowl with clingfilm and refrigerate for 30 minutes.

Remove from the fridge and spoon the batter into the prepared moulds, filling each mould halfway. Tap the tin on the work surface to eliminate air bubbles. Bake for 12 minutes or until the madeleines are puffed and the edges are golden. Remove from the oven and leave to cool in the tin for 5 minutes. Turn out onto a wire rack to cool. Using a pastry brush, coat the ridged side of each madeleine with the glaze. Madeleines can be stored in a single layer in an airtight container for up to three days.

**To make the orange glaze:** Mix the icing sugar, orange rind and juice in a small bowl until smooth.

**Quick change:** For chocolate madeleines, substitute 40 g cocoa powder for 2 ml ground cardamom. Do not ice – dust with 50 ml icing sugar.

# Fruity Friands
Makes 10

110 g cake flour

200 g castor sugar

6 jumbo egg whites

200 g butter, melted

100 g (250 ml) ground almonds

10 ml vanilla essence

5 fresh strawberries, hulled and halved

10 fresh cherries, pitted

icing sugar, for dusting

Preheat oven to 190 °C.

Coat a friand tin with cooking spray and set aside. Beat the flour, castor sugar and egg whites in a food mixer until smooth. Add the butter, almonds and vanilla essence, and mix. Spoon the batter into the friand moulds, filling each mould close to the top. Place half a strawberry and a cherry into the batter and bake for 25 minutes or until a skewer inserted into the centre comes out clean. Remove from the oven and leave to cool in the moulds for 10 minutes. Turn out onto a wire rack to cool. Dust with the icing sugar. Friands are at their best when made on the day of serving but can be stored in an airtight container for up to two days.

If strawberries and cherries are out of season, substitute with frozen strawberries and canned pitted cherries.

# Mini Gingerbreads

Makes 12

200 g unsalted butter

200 g (250 ml) caramel brown sugar

50 ml golden syrup

2 jumbo eggs

240 g self-raising flour

10 ml ground ginger

1 ml salt

200 ml milk

**Ginger Glaze**

150 g icing sugar

15 ml fresh lemon juice

30 g (50 ml) chopped glacé ginger

Preheat the oven to 190 °C.

Coat twelve 8 x 5 cm mini loaf tins with cooking spray and set aside. Cream the butter and sugar in a food mixer until light and creamy in colour. Add the syrup and eggs. Sift the flour, ginger and salt into a bowl and add alternately with the milk to the butter mixture. Mix thoroughly. Spoon the batter into the prepared tins and bake for 25 minutes or until a skewer inserted into the centre comes out clean. Remove from the oven and leave to cool in the tins for 10 minutes. Turn out onto a wire rack to cool.

**To make the ginger glaze:** Mix together the sugar, juice and ginger, and spoon over the loaves.

# Mini Christmas Cakes

Makes 6 jumbo muffins

1 x 440 g can crushed pineapple

100 g (125 ml) white sugar

150 g (250 ml) fruit cake mix

50 ml cooking oil

5 ml vanilla essence

200 g cake flour

1 ml salt

5 ml baking powder

5 ml bicarbonate of soda

5 ml mixed spice

icing sugar, for dusting

Preheat the oven to 180 °C.

Coat a six-hole jumbo muffin tin with cooking spray and set aside. Place the pineapple, sugar, cake mix and oil in a large, heavy-based saucepan and bring to the boil, stirring continuously. Remove from the heat and set aside to cool. Mix in the vanilla essence. Sift the flour, salt, baking powder, bicarbonate of soda and mixed spice into a bowl, then add to the fruit mixture. Spoon the batter into the prepared tin to two-thirds full and bake for 30 minutes or until a skewer inserted into the centre comes out clean. Remove from the oven and leave to cool in the tin for 10 minutes. Turn out onto a wire rack to cool. Dust with icing sugar.

# *Blissful* Biscuits

*An on-the-go crunch or a relaxing dunk – there's a favourite for everyone.*

# Baking Biscuits

I always set one week in a month aside and spend part of each day making a couple of batches of biscuits. Winter is a fabulous time to do so! I often double or treble the recipe and always make the recipes with the same method on the same day.

The biscuit recipes in this chapter use the Rubbing-in method as in Shortbread, the Creaming method as in Monte Carlos, the Melting method as in Brandy Snaps and the Whisking method as in Macaroons.

Biscuits keep very well, provided they are stored correctly in an airtight container. Biscuits also freeze successfully for up to one month. I also freeze the unbaked dough for up to three weeks and defrost in the fridge prior to shaping and baking.

# Florentine Wedges

Makes 30

400 g dark chocolate
300 g (500 ml) sultanas
160 g (4 x 250 ml) crushed cornflakes
100 g (250 ml) roasted unsalted peanuts
200 g red glacé cherries, chopped
1 x 385 g can condensed milk

Preheat the oven to 180 °C.

Line a 30 x 20 cm lamington tin with aluminium foil, extending the foil 5 cm over the edge of the tin. Coat the foil with cooking spray and set aside. Melt the chocolate in the top of a double boiler over simmering water or in a microwave oven until melted, spread evenly over the base of the lined tin and leave to set. Combine the sultanas, cornflakes, peanuts, chopped cherries and condensed milk in a bowl and mix thoroughly. Spread the mixture evenly over the chocolate base and bake for 20 minutes. Remove from the oven and set aside to cool. Refrigerate and cut into wedges or triangles. Florentines will keep in an airtight container for up to 10 days.

# Spicy Date and Ginger Squares

Makes 24

200 g pitted dates, chopped

250 ml milk

5 ml bicarbonate of soda

125 g butter or margarine

220 g castor sugar

200 ml golden syrup

2 jumbo eggs

15 ml ground ginger

5 ml ground allspice

280 g (500 ml) cake flour, sifted

**Icing**

100 g butter or margarine

2.5 ml ground ginger

15 ml golden syrup

250 g icing sugar, sifted

20 ml fresh lemon juice

Preheat the oven to 180 °C.

Line the base of a 30 x 20 cm lamington tin with baking paper. Coat the tin with cooking spray and set aside. Place the dates and milk in a small, heavy-based saucepan and bring to the boil. Remove from the heat, add the bicarbonate of soda and set aside for 10 minutes. Beat the butter or margarine and castor sugar in a food mixer until light and creamy in colour. Add the syrup and eggs, one at a time, beating thoroughly after each addition. Mix in the spices and flour thoroughly. Spoon the date mixture into the flour mixture, and mix. Pour the mixture into the prepared tin and bake for 30 minutes or until a skewer inserted into the centre comes out clean. Remove from the oven and leave to cool in the tin for 15 minutes.

**To make the icing:** Beat the butter or margarine, ginger and syrup in a food mixer until smooth. Gradually add the icing sugar, beating thoroughly after each addition. Stir in the lemon juice.

**To assemble:** Spread the icing over the cooled biscuit and cut into 5 cm squares. The squares will keep in an airtight container for up to one week.

# Lemon and Lime Coconut Slices

Makes 24

125 g butter or margarine

60 g castor sugar

150 g cake flour

60 g desiccated coconut

100 ml lime or orange marmalade, warmed

**Topping**

100 g butter or margarine

75 g castor sugar

10 ml grated lemon rind

10 ml grated lime rind

2 jumbo eggs

160 g (500 ml) desiccated coconut

50 g cake flour

Preheat the oven to 200 °C.

Line the base of a 30 x 20 cm lamington tin with baking paper. Coat the tin with cooking spray and set aside. Cream the butter or margarine and castor sugar in a food mixer fitted with the plastic blade until light and creamy in colour. Stir in the flour and coconut, and mix thoroughly. Press the mixture evenly over the base of the prepared tin and bake for 12 minutes. Remove from the oven, spread with the warm marmalade and set aside.

**To make the topping:** Reduce the oven temperature to 180 °C. Cream the butter or margarine, castor sugar and the rinds in a food mixer until light and fluffy. Add the eggs one at a time, beating well after each addition. Stir in the coconut and flour. Spoon the topping over the marmalade in the tin and bake for 20 minutes. Remove from the oven and leave to cool in the tin. Cut into 4 cm wide oblong slices. The slices will keep in an airtight container for up to three days.

# Peach and Almond Slices

Makes 16

200 g cake flour

30 ml castor sugar

100 g butter or margarine

1 jumbo egg

**Topping**

150 g butter or margarine

165 g castor sugar

1 jumbo egg

60 g cake flour

165 g (375 ml) ground almonds

5 ml vanilla essence

3 fresh peaches, peeled, stoned and sliced

100 ml smooth apricot jam, warmed for glazing

Preheat the oven to 180 °C.

Line the base of a 30 x 20 cm lamington tin with baking paper. Coat the tin with cooking spray and set aside. Mix the flour, castor sugar and butter or margarine in a food mixer fitted with the plastic blade until the mixture resembles breadcrumbs. Add the egg. Press the mixture evenly into the prepared tin and bake for 12 minutes. Remove from the oven and set aside to cool.

**To make the topping:** Cream the butter or margarine and castor sugar in a food mixer until light and creamy in colour. Add the egg, flour, almonds and vanilla essence, and mix thoroughly. Spread the filling evenly over the biscuit base and bake for 15 minutes. Top with the peach slices and bake for 10–15 minutes. Remove from the oven and brush with the apricot jam. Cool in the tin, then cut into slices. The slices will keep in an airtight container in the fridge for up to three days.

# Chocolate-dipped Shortbread
Makes 24

500 g butter

350 g cake flour

170 g (325 ml) icing sugar

120 g (250 ml) cornflour

80 g (250 ml) desiccated coconut

5 ml vanilla essence

200 g dark chocolate, melted

Preheat the oven to 180 °C.

Grease a 30 x 20 cm lamington tin with butter, sprinkle with flour and set aside. Cream the butter in a food mixer until light and creamy in colour. Add the flour, icing sugar, cornflour and coconut. Mix thoroughly, then add the vanilla essence. Press the dough into the prepared tin and prick with a fork. The dough should be about 2.5 cm thick, as these biscuits are at their best when not too thin. Bake for 40–45 minutes. Remove from the oven and set aside to cool. Cut into squares.

**To assemble:** Dip a corner of each square into the melted chocolate and place on a wire rack until the chocolate hardens. The shortbread will keep in an airtight container for up to one week.

# Belgian Shortbread
Makes 18

200 g white sugar

280 g (500 ml) self-raising flour

1 ml salt

150 g butter

1 jumbo egg

100 ml raspberry jam

350 g pitted dates, quartered

50 g (125 ml) roasted unsalted peanuts

15 ml castor sugar

Preheat the oven to 150 °C.

Coat a 30 x 20 cm lamington tin with cooking spray and set aside. Combine the sugar, flour and salt in a large mixing bowl and rub in the butter until the mixture resembles breadcrumbs. Add the egg. Shape the dough into a ball and cut in half. Press one half of the dough into the prepared tin. Spread the jam over the surface and cover with the dates. Grate the remaining dough over the dates and press the peanuts into the pastry. Sprinkle with the castor sugar. Bake for 1 hour. Allow to cool, then cut into fingers to serve. The shortbread will keep in an airtight container for up to one week.

# Monte Carlos

Makes 24 sandwiched biscuits

370 g butter or margarine

200 g (250 ml) golden brown sugar

2 jumbo eggs

5 ml vanilla essence

340 g self-raising flour

225 g cake flour

80 g (250 ml) desiccated coconut

**Filling**

120 g butter or margarine

200 g icing sugar, sifted

2.5 ml vanilla essence

10 ml milk

10 ml grated orange rind

125 ml strawberry or apricot jam

Preheat the oven to 180 °C.

Coat two baking sheets with cooking spray and set aside.

1  Cream the butter or margarine and brown sugar in a food mixer fitted with the plastic blade until light and creamy in colour.

2  Add the eggs and vanilla essence.

3  Sift the flours into a mixing bowl.

4  Add the flour to the margarine mixture.

5  Mix in the coconut.

6  Place small balls of dough on the prepared sheets.

7  Flatten with a fork.

8  Bake for 12 minutes or until golden brown in colour.

9  Remove from the oven and turn out onto a wire rack to cool.

**To make the filling**

10  Cream the butter or margarine and icing sugar in a food mixer fitted with the plastic blade until light and fluffy.

11  Add the vanilla essence, milk and orange rind, and mix thoroughly.

**To assemble**

12  Sandwich the biscuit halves together with the filling and jam, and store in an airtight container for up to one week.

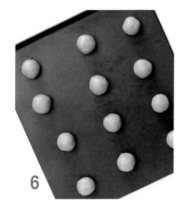

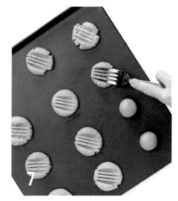

# Brandy Snaps

Makes 20

100 g butter

100 g castor sugar

60 ml golden syrup

5 ml brandy

100 g cake flour

5 ml ground ginger

**Filling**

500 ml fresh cream

50 g chopped preserved ginger
   in syrup, drained

Preheat the oven to 160 °C.

Line two baking sheets with baking paper and set aside.

1   Place the butter, castor sugar, syrup and brandy in a small, heavy-based saucepan and melt over low heat. Do not allow to boil.

2   Stir in the flour and ginger until smooth.

3   Remove from the heat.

4   Drop teaspoonfuls of the mixture onto the prepared sheets, allowing sufficient space in between for spreading.

5   Bake for 8–9 minutes or until golden brown in colour.

6   Remove from the oven and set aside to cool slightly.

7   Using a spatula, lift each brandy snap from the sheet.

8   Wrap around the handle of a wooden spoon.

9   Once firm, remove from the spoon and place on a cooling rack to harden.

**To assemble**

10   Whip the cream until stiff, then stir in the ginger.

11   Fill each brandy snap with the ginger cream.

If the brandy snaps harden before you've managed to roll them, pop them back into the oven for 10 seconds to soften.

## Crispy Cinnamon Biscuits

*Makes 48*

180 g butter or margarine
300 g (375 ml) white sugar
2 jumbo eggs
400 g cake flour
10 ml cream of tartar
5 ml bicarbonate of soda
2.5 ml salt
30 ml white sugar
10 ml ground cinnamon

Preheat the oven to 200 °C.

Cream the butter or margarine, sugar and eggs in a food mixer fitted with the plastic blade until light and creamy in colour. Sift the flour, cream of tartar, bicarbonate of soda and salt into a mixing bowl, then spoon into the egg mixture. Mix together. Place the dough in the fridge for 1 hour. Remove the dough from the fridge and roll into balls the size of walnuts. Combine the sugar and cinnamon in a small bowl. Roll each ball of dough in the sugar coating mixture. Place the dough balls on ungreased baking sheets about 2.5 cm apart. Bake for 8–10 minutes or until light brown in colour, but still soft. Remove from the oven and turn out onto a wire rack to cool.

Do not store biscuits in a tin with other cakes, as they will lose their crispness. If this happens, place the biscuits in a preheated oven at 200 °C for 3–5 minutes to crisp.

# Macaroon Rounds with Praline Cream

Makes 6 sandwiched macaroons

120 g ground almonds

200 g castor sugar

10 ml cake flour

2 jumbo egg whites

2.5 ml almond essence

30 ml flaked almonds

2 fresh mangoes, peeled and sliced or

　　1 x 410 g can mango slices, drained

icing sugar, for dusting

**Praline Cream**

110 g castor sugar

30 ml water

1 ml baking powder

60 g whole blanched almonds, toasted

200 g ricotta cheese, drained

80 g icing sugar

200 ml thick fresh cream

Preheat the oven to 180 °C.

Line a baking sheet with baking paper and trace twelve 8 cm diameter circles onto the paper. Coat the paper with cooking spray and set aside. Combine the almonds, castor sugar and flour in a food mixer fitted with the plastic blade and mix thoroughly. Add the egg whites and almond essence, and beat until combined. Spread the macaroon mixture within the traced circles, leaving a 1 cm border, and sprinkle the mixture with the flaked almonds. Bake for 15 minutes. Remove from the oven and cool for 10 minutes. Using a palette knife, transfer the rounds to a wire rack.

**To make the praline cream:** Line a baking sheet with baking paper. Coat the paper with cooking spray and set aside. Combine the castor sugar and water in a small, heavy-based saucepan, heat and stir until the sugar dissolves. Bring to the boil and boil without stirring until golden in colour. Remove from the heat, add the baking powder and almonds, and stir. Pour onto the prepared sheet and cool until firm. Break the praline into pieces, grind coarsely in a food mixer fitted with the metal blade and set aside. Mix the ricotta and icing sugar in the food mixer, now fitted with the plastic blade, until smooth. Transfer the mixture to a bowl, add the cream and praline, and mix. Cover and refrigerate until ready to use.

**To assemble:** Spread a teaspoon of the praline cream onto the base of a macaroon. Top with mango slices and another macaroon base, and dust with icing sugar. Unfilled macaroons will keep in an airtight container for up to two days. Once filled, eat on the same day.

# Chocolate Chunk Brownies

Makes 24

180 g butter or margarine

200 g milk chocolate, coarsely chopped

300 g dark chocolate, coarsely chopped

380 g golden brown sugar

6 jumbo eggs

5 ml vanilla essence

280 g (500 ml) cake flour, sifted

2.5 ml salt

5 ml baking powder

2.5 ml ground cinnamon

icing sugar, for decorating

Preheat the oven to 180 °C.

Line a 33 x 22 cm lamington tin with baking paper. Coat the tin with cooking spray and set aside. Melt the butter or margarine in a large, heavy-based saucepan. Add the milk chocolate and dark chocolate, stirring until melted. Add the brown sugar and stir until dissolved. Remove the saucepan from the heat and set aside to cool. Beat the eggs and vanilla essence in a large mixing bowl and add the flour, salt, baking powder and cinnamon. Add the chocolate mixture to the flour mixture, beating thoroughly with a wooden spoon. Spoon the mixture into the prepared tin and smooth the top using a spatula. Bake for 25 minutes or until a skewer inserted into the centre comes out clean. Remove from the oven and allow to cool completely in the tin. Cut into squares and decorate with icing sugar.

**Handy hint:** For evenly cut brownies, refrigerate before cutting.

# White Chocolate and Almond Biscotti

Makes 30

280 g (500 ml) cake flour

2.5 ml baking powder

1 ml salt

220 g castor sugar

100 g unsalted butter

125 g ground almonds

100 g white chocolate, melted in the
microwave at 100% power for 2 minutes

2 jumbo egg yolks

2 jumbo eggs

10 ml vanilla essence

15 ml sweet marsala

Preheat the oven to 180 °C.

Line a baking sheet with baking paper. Coat the sheet with cooking spray and set aside. Sift the flour, baking powder and salt into a large mixing bowl and stir in the castor sugar. Rub in the butter until the mixture resembles breadcrumbs. Stir in the almonds and chocolate. Whisk the egg yolks, eggs, vanilla essence and marsala in a mixing bowl, and stir into the flour mixture. Combine to form a scone-like dough. Turn the dough out onto a lightly floured surface and shape into a 20 x 8 x 2 cm rectangle. Lift the dough onto the prepared sheet, cover with clingfilm and refrigerate overnight. Remove the clingfilm and bake on the same sheet for 35 minutes or until a skewer inserted into the centre comes out clean. Cool completely. Using a serrated knife cut into 1.5 cm thick slices. Reduce the oven temperature to 100 °C. Arrange the biscotti on a baking paper-lined baking sheet and place in the oven to dry for 1 hour or until very lightly browned. Transfer to a wire rack to cool. Biscotti will keep in an airtight container for up to two weeks.

# White Panforte

Makes 1 cake

200 g (500 ml) whole blanched almonds,
    coarsely chopped
200 g (500 ml) whole hazelnuts,
    coarsely chopped
100 g mixed citrus peel, coarsely chopped
100 g dried pineapple, coarsely chopped
150 g (250 ml) glacé figs, coarsely chopped
100 g cake flour, sifted
2.5 ml ground coriander
5 ml ground cinnamon
5 ml ground mixed spice
200 g castor sugar
200 ml honey

Preheat the oven to 160 °C.

Line the base of a 24 cm round springform tin with baking paper. Coat the tin with cooking spray and set aside. Combine the almonds, hazelnuts, citrus peel, pineapple, figs, flour and spices in a large mixing bowl, and set aside. Place the castor sugar and honey in a small, heavy-based saucepan and bring to the boil. Pour the honey syrup mixture over the fruit mixture and stir to combine. The mixture will not be completely coated. Set aside to coo,l then spoon the mixture into the prepared tin. Bake for 1 hour or until slightly puffed. Remove from the oven and cool in the tin for 20 minutes. Turn out onto a wire rack to cool. Serve in thin slices. Panforte will keep wrapped in clingfilm in an airtight container for up to one month.

# Chocolate Creams

Makes 24 sandwiched biscuits

250 g butter or margarine
140 g white sugar
250 g cake flour
5 ml baking powder
2.5 ml salt
45 ml cocoa powder
125 g desiccated coconut
100 ml boiling water

**Filling**
450 g icing sugar
200 g butter or margarine, softened
5 ml vanilla essence
30 ml cocoa powder
10 ml milk

icing sugar and cocoa powder, for dusting

Preheat the oven to 200 °C.

Line two baking sheets with baking paper. Coat the sheets with cooking spray and set aside. Cream the butter or margarine and sugar in a food mixer fitted with the plastic blade. Sift the flour, baking powder, salt and cocoa into a bowl and add to the butter mixture. Mix in the coconut and boiling water. Spoon the dough into a piping bag fitted with a large star nozzle. Pipe stars 2.5 cm in diameter onto the prepared sheet and bake for 12–13 minutes. Remove from the oven and turn out onto a wire rack to cool.

**To make the filling:** Beat the icing sugar and butter or margarine in a food mixer until creamy. Add the vanilla essence, cocoa and milk, and beat until mixed.

**To assemble:** Sandwich the Romany Cream stars together with a teaspoon of icing and dust with a mixture of icing sugar and cocoa powder.

# Condensed Milk Biscuits
Makes 48

250 g butter or margarine

160 g white sugar

1 x 285 g can condensed milk

420 g (750 ml) cake flour

10 ml baking powder

2.5 ml salt

5 ml vanilla essence

Preheat the oven to 190 °C.

Cream the butter or margarine and sugar in a food mixer fitted with the plastic blade until light and creamy in colour. Stir in the condensed milk. Sift the flour, baking powder and salt into a bowl and add to the margarine mixture. Add the vanilla essence and mix thoroughly. Roll the dough into small balls, place onto ungreased baking sheets 2.5 cm apart and flatten with a fork. Bake for 15 minutes or until golden brown in colour. Remove from the oven and turn out onto a wire rack to cool.

# Perfect Ginger Biscuits
Makes 48

180 g butter or margarine

180 g white sugar

250 ml golden syrup

45 ml ground ginger

10 ml bicarbonate of soda

25 ml milk

560 g (4 x 250 ml) cake flour

5 ml salt

Preheat the oven to 190 °C.

Coat two baking sheets with cooking spray and set aside. Cream the butter or margarine, sugar, syrup and ginger together in a food mixer fitted with the plastic blade. Dissolve the bicarbonate of soda in the milk and add to the margarine mixture. Sift the flour and salt into a bowl and add to the margarine mixture. Mix thoroughly. Roll the dough into balls and place 2.5 cm apart on the prepared baking sheets. Flatten the biscuits with the thumb and bake for 10–12 minutes or until golden brown in colour. Remove from the oven and turn out onto a wire rack to cool.

# Pecan Nut Biscuits

Makes 24

250 g butter

65 g (125 ml) icing sugar

250 g pecan nuts, chopped

10 ml cold water

5 ml vanilla essence

280 g (500 ml) cake flour

10 ml baking powder

60 ml icing sugar, for coating

Preheat the oven to 160 °C.

Coat a baking sheet with cooking spray and set aside. Cream the butter and 65 g icing sugar in a food mixer fitted with the plastic blade. Add the nuts, water and vanilla essence. Sift the flour and baking powder into a bowl and add to the butter mixture. Mix thoroughly. Shape the dough into oblongs and place onto the prepared baking sheet. Bake for 20 minutes. Remove from the oven and, while still warm, coat with the 60 ml icing sugar and set aside on a wire rack to cool.

# Buttermilk Rusks

Makes 48

1.5 kg self-raising flour

300 g (375 ml) white sugar

10 ml salt

500 g butter or margarine, melted

500 ml buttermilk

3 jumbo eggs

Preheat the oven to 200 °C.

Coat three 28 x 11 cm loaf tins with cooking spray and set aside. Combine the flour, sugar and salt in a large mixing bowl. Add the remaining ingredients and knead until combined. Shape the dough into balls and place two balls side by side in rows into the prepared tins. Bake for 30 minutes. Reduce the oven temperature to 180 °C and bake for a further 30 minutes or until a skewer inserted into the centre comes out clean. Turn out onto a wire rack to cool. Break the rusks apart. Dry out in the oven at 100 °C or in the warming drawer of the oven for 6–8 hours.

# Nutty Wholewheat Rusks

Makes 48

1 kg wholewheat flour

280 g (500 ml) cake flour

200 g (250 ml) caramel brown sugar

5 ml salt

10 ml baking powder

5 ml bicarbonate of soda

5 ml cream of tartar

150 g (250 ml) seedless raisins

150 g (250 ml) pecan nuts, chopped

50 ml sesame seeds

250 g butter or margarine, melted

500 ml low-fat plain yoghurt

2 jumbo eggs

200 ml cooking oil

Preheat the oven to 180 °C.

Coat three 28 x 11 cm loaf tins with cooking spray and set aside. Combine the flours, sugar, salt, baking powder, bicarbonate of soda and cream of tartar in a large mixing bowl. Add the remaining ingredients and knead until combined. Shape the dough into balls and place two balls side by side in rows into the prepared tins. Bake for 1 hour or until a skewer inserted into the centre comes out clean. Turn out onto a wire rack to cool. Break the rusks apart, then dry out in the oven at 100 °C or in the warming drawer of the oven for 6–8 hours.

# Munch *Time*

*When temptation beckons, succumb to these*
*perfect in-betweeners.*

# Creating Cupcakes

Cupcakes are very much in vogue. Brides often prefer a cupcake wedding cake to the more traditional fruit wedding cake. Once you have a good basic cupcake mixture, it is so easy to vary the taste by adding a different flavouring or using a different icing or decoration. I always keep a batch of un-iced cupcakes in the freezer. Cupcakes defrost in a jiffy and take only a few minutes to coat with an icing. Children can stay amused for hours with a batch of cupcakes, bowls of coloured icing and some sprinkles!

# Scone Secrets

Scone dough is mixed briefly and lightly. The dry ingredients are sifted to incorporate as much air as possible. Rubbing the butter into the dry ingredients also aerates the dough. Once the liquid is added, the raising agent becomes active. A good scone dough is always slightly sticky to the touch. Scones are best eaten warm on the day they are baked. Scones freeze successfully for up to one month – wrap individually in clingfilm and place in a freezer bag. Reheat in a preheated oven at 180 °C for 8 minutes.

# Making Muffins

Sweet or savoury muffins are so versatile – enjoy them for breakfast, lunch, dinner or snacks! Muffins can be mixed by hand in a large mixing bowl or in a food mixer. The batter should be mixed quickly, as overmixing will result in chewy muffins that are full of holes. To equalise the baking time, fill any unfilled holes in the muffin tin with water. Muffins are best eaten warm on the day they are baked. They freeze successfully for up to one month if individually wrapped in clingfilm and placed in a freezer bag. Reheat in the microwave at 100% power for 1 minute.

# Two-tone Coffee Cupcakes

Makes 20

15 ml instant coffee granules

15 ml boiling water

200 g self-raising flour

150 g cake flour

5 ml baking powder

200 g castor sugar

150 g butter or margarine

200 ml milk

3 jumbo eggs

5 ml vanilla essence

**Glaze**

150 g icing sugar

30 ml cocoa powder

20 ml water

**Coffee Butter Icing**

15 ml instant coffee granules

15 ml boiling water

150 g butter or margarine

200 g icing sugar

20 ml milk

Preheat the oven to 180 °C.

Line muffin tins with paper cases and set aside. Dissolve the coffee in the boiling water and set aside to cool. Place the flours, baking powder, castor sugar, butter or margarine, milk, eggs and vanilla essence in a food mixer and beat thoroughly until combined. Add the coffee mixture, beating thoroughly. Spoon the mixture into the prepared tins, filling each paper case three-quarters full. Bake for 20–25 minutes until the tops of the cupcakes spring back when lightly touched. Leave to cool in the tins for 10 minutes, then turn out onto a wire rack to cool.

**To make the glaze:** Mix together the icing sugar, cocoa and water in a small bowl. Spread on top of each cupcake.

**To make the coffee butter icing:** Dissolve the coffee in the boiling water and set aside to cool. Beat the butter or margarine and icing sugar in a food mixer fitted with the plastic blade. Add the milk and coffee. Spoon into a piping bag fitted with a star-shaped nozzle and pipe stars onto the top of each glazed cupcake.

# Carmen's Double Chocolate Cupcakes

Makes 30

250 ml fresh cream

400 g dark chocolate

5 jumbo eggs

160 g castor sugar

140 g (250 ml) cake flour

15 ml cocoa powder

5 ml baking powder

**Chocolate Topping**

100 g dark chocolate, broken into pieces

100 ml fresh cream

sugared cake decorations

Preheat the oven to 180 °C.

Line muffin tins with paper cases and set aside. Place the cream and chocolate in a small, heavy-based saucepan over low heat and stir until smooth. Cool slightly. Place the eggs and castor sugar in a food mixer and beat until light and creamy in colour. Beat in the chocolate mixture. Sift the flour, cocoa and baking powder into a mixing bowl and add to the chocolate mixture. Mix until combined using a metal spoon. Spoon the mixture into the prepared tins, filling each paper case three-quarters full. Bake for 20 minutes or until a skewer inserted into the centre comes out clean. Set aside to cool completely.

**To make the chocolate topping:** Melt the chocolate and cream in the top part of a double boiler over simmering water. Remove from the heat and stir until smooth. Cool slightly. Spread the topping over the cupcakes and decorate with sugared cake decorations.

# Little Fairy Cakes

Makes 24

200 g self-raising flour

140 g (250 ml) cake flour

200 g castor sugar

5 ml baking powder

150 g butter or margarine

200 ml milk

3 jumbo eggs

5 ml vanilla essence

coloured sugar crystals, for coating

100 ml strawberry or raspberry jam

200 ml fresh cream, whipped

Preheat the oven to 180 °C.

Line muffin tins with paper cases and set aside. Place the flours, castor sugar, baking powder, butter or margarine, milk, eggs and vanilla essence in a food mixer and beat until the mixture is light and creamy in colour. Spoon into the prepared tins, filling each paper case three-quarters full. Bake for 15–20 minutes or until golden brown in colour. Leave to cool in the tins for 5 minutes, then turn out onto a wire rack to cool for 30 minutes.

**To assemble:** Place the coloured sugar crystals on a plate. Warm the jam in the microwave and set aside. Cut a shallow round from the top of each cupcake. Cut in half, brush each piece with jam and coat with the coloured sugar crystals. Place a dollop of whipped cream on each cupcake and position the two coated pieces in the cream to form wings.

# Cream Cheese Cupcakes with a Berry Swirl

Makes 12

250 ml (about 10) finely ground Oreo®
   or Romany Cream® biscuits

50 g butter, melted

100 g frozen strawberries
   or raspberries, thawed

30 ml icing sugar, sifted

375 g smooth cream cheese

100 g castor sugar

3 jumbo eggs

5 ml vanilla essence

6 fresh strawberries, halved

icing sugar, for dusting

Preheat the oven to 170 °C.

Line a 12-hole muffin tin with paper cases and set aside. Combine the ground biscuits and butter in a small bowl. Line the base of the paper cases with the crumb mixture and bake for 5 minutes. Remove from the oven and set aside to cool. Mash the strawberries or raspberries to a pulp with the back of a fork and stir in the icing sugar. Set aside. Place the cream cheese in a food mixer, add the castor sugar and the eggs, one at a time, beating well after each addition. Add the vanilla essence. Spoon the cheese mixture over the biscuit bases. Place 5 ml berry purée on top of the cheese mixture and, using a skewer, swirl through the cheese mixture. Bake for 15 minutes or until set. Leave the oven door ajar and allow the cakes to cool completely in the switched-off oven. Top with a strawberry half and a dusting of icing sugar.

# Butterfly Cupcakes

Makes 12

150 g butter

160 g castor sugar

3 jumbo eggs

5 ml vanilla essence

200 g self-raising flour, sifted

100 ml milk

100 ml strawberry jam, warmed

250 ml fresh cream, whipped

6 fresh strawberries, hulled and quartered

50 ml icing sugar, for dusting

Preheat the oven to 180 °C.

Line a 12-hole muffin tin with paper cases and set aside. Cream the butter, castor sugar, eggs and vanilla essence together in a food mixer and beat until light and creamy in colour. Add the flour alternately with the milk and beat until mixed. Spoon the mixture into the prepared tin, filling each paper case three-quarters full. Bake for 15 minutes or until a skewer inserted into the centre comes out clean. Leave to cool in the tin for 5 minutes, then turn out onto a wire rack to cool for 30 minutes.

**To assemble:** Using a serrated knife, cut a shallow round from the top of each cupcake. Halve the rounds to make two wings. Fill the space where the round has been removed with jam and cream. Position the wings on top of the cupcake. Add the strawberry pieces and dust with a little icing sugar.

# Apple Streusel Cupcakes

Makes 12

200 g cake flour

7.5 ml baking powder

1 ml salt

90 g butter

200 g (250 ml) white sugar

2 jumbo eggs

2.5 ml vanilla essence

1 green apple, peeled, cored and diced

100 ml milk

**Streusel Topping**

80 g caramel brown sugar

5 ml ground cinnamon

50 g butter

50 ml icing sugar, for dusting

Preheat the oven to 180 °C.

Line a 12-hole muffin tin with paper cases and set aside. Sift the flour, baking powder and salt into a mixing bowl and set aside. Beat the butter, sugar, eggs and vanilla essence in a food mixer until smooth. Add the flour mixture. Mix in the apple and milk, and beat thoroughly. Spoon the mixture into the prepared tin, filling each paper case halfway, and set aside.

**To make the streusel topping:** Combine the brown sugar and cinnamon in a small bowl, and rub in the butter until the mixture holds together in small, moist clumps. Sprinkle the streusel mixture onto the mixture in the paper cases and spoon in the remaining cupcake mixture. Bake for 20 minutes or until the tops of the cupcakes spring back when lightly touched. Remove from the oven and leave to cool in the tin for 5 minutes. Turn out onto a wire rack to cool completely before dusting with the icing sugar.

# Tropical Cupcakes
Makes 12

75 ml dried pineapple, finely chopped

75 ml dried mango or papino, finely chopped

50 ml coconut rum

200 g cake flour

5 ml baking powder

2.5 ml bicarbonate of soda

1 ml salt

100 g butter

200 g (250 ml) white sugar

3 jumbo egg whites

45 g macadamia nuts, toasted
      and coarsely chopped

200 ml buttermilk

50 ml icing sugar, for dusting

Preheat the oven to 180 °C.

Line a 12-hole muffin tin with paper cases and set aside. Combine the pineapple, mango and rum in a bowl and microwave at 100% power for 3 minutes or until the fruit is soft and hot. Set aside to cool. Sift the flour, baking powder, bicarbonate of soda and salt into a bowl and set aside. Cream the butter and sugar together in a food mixer until light and creamy in colour. Add the egg whites, nuts and buttermilk alternately with the sifted dry ingredients to the butter mixture. Mix in the fruit mixture. Spoon the batter into the prepared tin, filling each paper case three-quarters full. Bake for 20 minutes or until the tops of the cupcakes spring back when lightly touched. Remove from the oven and leave to cool in the tin for 10 minutes. Turn out onto a wire rack to cool. Dust with the icing sugar.

# Ice-cream Cone Cupcakes
Makes 12

12 flat-bottomed ice-cream cones

150 g butter or margarine

160 g castor sugar

3 jumbo eggs

5 ml vanilla essence

200 g self-raising flour, sifted

100 ml milk

1 x quantity Rich Butter Icing (see page 218)

red Astros™, for decorating

Preheat the oven to 180 °C.

Line a 12-hole muffin tin with the flat-bottomed ice-cream cones and set aside. Cream the butter or margarine, castor sugar, eggs and vanilla essence together in a food mixer and beat until light and creamy in colour. Mix the flour alternately with the milk into the margarine mixture and beat thoroughly. Fill each cone three-quarters full with the mixture. Bake for 20–25 minutes or until the tops of the cupcakes are golden brown and a skewer inserted into the centre comes out clean. Remove from the oven and leave to cool in the tin for 10 minutes. Turn out onto a wire rack to cool. Ice with Rich Butter Icing and decorate with red Astros™.

# Traditional Scones

Makes 12

450 g self-raising flour

5 ml salt

100 g butter or margarine

300 ml milk

1 jumbo egg yolk beaten with 25 ml water

Preheat the oven to 200 °C.

Coat a baking sheet with cooking spray and set aside.

1   Sift the flour and salt into a large mixing bowl.
2   Cut the butter or margarine into the flour.
3   Rub in the butter or margarine until the mixture resembles breadcrumbs.
4   Make a well in the centre, add the milk and mix to form a soft dough.
5   Gather the dough together with the fingers and turn out onto a lightly floured surface.
6   Knead lightly until the dough is smooth and free from cracks.
7   Roll out to a 12 mm-thick round. Turn the dough 90° to the left after each rolling.

8   Using a 5 cm floured cutter, cut out the scones. Press the cutter firmly into the dough, but do not twist.
9   Place the scones on the prepared sheet 2.5 cm apart, brush with the egg wash and bake for 15 minutes.
10  Remove from the oven and turn out onto a wire rack to cool.

**Handy hint:** If using plain cake flour add 30 ml baking powder.

4 7 8 9

# Fabulous Tea Scones

Makes 15

650 g cake flour
30 ml baking powder
10 ml white sugar
5 ml salt

240 g butter
2 jumbo eggs
250 ml milk
1 jumbo egg yolk, beaten, for glazing

Preheat the oven to 180 °C.

Coat a baking sheet with cooking spray and set aside. Sift the dry ingredients into a large mixing bowl. Make a well in the centre, cut the butter into the flour and rub in until the mixture resembles breadcrumbs. Stir in the eggs and milk, and mix to form a soft dough. Turn out onto a lightly floured surface and knead into a rectangular shape. Roll the dough until 2.5 cm thick and, using a knife, cut into 15 squares. Place the scones in three rows of five on the prepared baking sheet and brush with the egg yolk. Bake for 25 minutes or until a skewer inserted into the centre comes out clean. Remove from the oven and turn out onto a wire rack to cool.

# Nut Scones

Makes 10–12

280 g (500 ml) cake flour
15 ml baking powder
2.5 ml salt
50 ml white sugar
120 g butter or margarine

50 g chopped pecan nuts, walnuts
    or hazelnuts
200 ml milk
30 ml cake flour

Preheat the oven to 200 °C.

Coat a baking sheet with cooking spray and set aside. Sift the flour, baking powder, salt and sugar into a large mixing bowl. Rub in the butter or margarine with the fingertips until the mixture resembles breadcrumbs, then mix in the nuts. Add the milk and, using a palette knife, mix to form a soft dough. Place the dough on a lightly floured surface, sprinkle with the 30 ml flour and toss lightly. Flatten the dough lightly by hand to about 1.5 cm thick and, using a 7.5 cm floured heart-shaped cutter, cut out the scones. Place on the prepared sheet. Bake for 20 minutes or until a skewer inserted into the centre comes out clean. Remove from the oven and turn out onto a wire rack to cool.

**Handy hint:** For a fruitier variation, add 60 g sultanas and 10 ml chopped mixed citrus peel to the nuts.

# Rich, Sweet Scones
Makes 6

| | |
|---|---|
| 280 g (500 ml) cake flour | 100 g butter |
| 20 ml baking powder | 1 jumbo egg, beaten |
| 1 ml salt | 250 ml sour cream |
| 15 ml white sugar | |

Preheat the oven to 200 °C.

Coat a six-hole jumbo muffin tin with cooking spray and set aside. Sift the flour, baking powder and salt into a large mixing bowl. Add the sugar. Rub the butter into the flour until the mixture resembles breadcrumbs, then mix in the egg and sour cream. Drop spoonfuls of the dough into the prepared tin and bake for 10–15 minutes or until a skewer inserted into the centre comes out clean. Remove from the oven and turn out onto a wire rack to cool. Serve with strawberry jam.

# Fruity Scone Round
Serves 6

| | |
|---|---|
| 225 g self-raising flour, sifted | **Glaze** |
| 2.5 ml salt | 15 ml honey |
| 50 g butter or margarine | 10 ml hot water |
| 25 ml castor sugar | |
| 50 g fruit cake mix | |
| 200 ml milk | |
| 50 ml cake flour | |

Preheat the oven to 220 °C.

Coat a baking sheet with cooking spray and set aside. Sift the flour and salt into a large mixing bowl. Rub the butter or margarine into the flour until the mixture resembles breadcrumbs. Stir in the castor sugar and fruit cake mix. Make a well in the centre, pour in the milk and stir to form a soft dough. Shape the dough into a ball with the fingertips and turn out onto a lightly floured surface. Knead the dough until smooth and free from cracks. Shape the dough into a single large 12 mm-thick round. Place the dough onto the prepared baking sheet. Dip the blade of a sharp knife into the 50 ml flour and mark the dough into six portions, but do not cut through the dough. Combine the honey and water in a small bowl and glaze the top of the round. Bake for 20–25 minutes or until a skewer inserted into the centre comes out clean. Remove from the oven and turn out onto a wire rack to cool. Pull the warm wedges of the scone round apart with the fingers.

# Wholewheat Breakfast Scones

Makes 4

260 g wholewheat flour

15 ml baking powder

1 ml salt

110 g butter or margarine

15 ml golden brown sugar

100 g pitted dates, chopped

100 ml milk

25 ml milk, for brushing

Preheat the oven to 200 °C.

Coat a baking sheet with cooking spray and set aside. Combine the flour, baking powder and salt in a large mixing bowl. Rub in the butter or margarine until the mixture resembles breadcrumbs. Add the brown sugar, dates and 100 ml milk, and mix. The dough will have a sticky, soft consistency. Shape the dough into a square and place onto the prepared baking sheet. Dip the blade of a sharp knife into flour and mark the dough into four squares. Brush with the milk. Bake for 25 minutes or until a skewer inserted into the centre comes out clean. Remove from the oven and turn out onto a wire rack to cool.

# Wholewheat Cheese Scones

Makes 9

140 g (250 ml) cake flour

15 ml baking powder

2.5 ml salt

10 ml white sugar

5 ml mustard powder

150 g (250 ml) wholewheat flour

80 g butter or margarine

100 g grated Cheddar cheese

1 jumbo egg

100 ml milk

1 jumbo egg yolk, beaten with 10 ml water

1 ml paprika

Preheat the oven to 200 °C.

Coat a baking sheet with cooking spray and set aside. Sift the flour, baking powder, salt, sugar and mustard powder into a large mixing bowl. Add the wholewheat flour. Rub in the butter or margarine until the mixture resembles breadcrumbs. Add the cheese, egg and milk. Using a fork, shape the dough into a square and turn out onto a lightly floured surface. Using a knife, cut into nine squares. Place the squares on the prepared sheet and brush with the egg wash. Sprinkle with the paprika and bake for 15 minutes or until a skewer inserted into the centre comes out clean. Remove from the oven and turn out onto a wire rack to cool. Serve warm with grated cheese on the side.

# Cheese Puffs

Makes 24

140 g (250 ml) cake flour

2.5 ml salt

20 ml baking powder

2.5 ml cayenne pepper

2.5 ml mustard powder

40 g butter or margarine

100 g grated mature Cheddar cheese

1 jumbo egg

200 ml milk

Preheat the oven to 200 °C.

Coat two 12-hole mini muffin tins with cooking spray and set aside. Sift the flour, salt, baking powder, cayenne pepper and mustard powder into a large mixing bowl. Mix in the butter or margarine, cheese, egg and milk. Spoon the mixture into the prepared tins, filling each hole three-quarters full. Bake for 12–15 minutes or until a skewer inserted into the centre comes out clean. Remove from the oven and turn out onto a wire rack to cool.

# Cheese Scones

Makes 8

These delicious savoury scones are so quick and easy to make you can even prepare them for breakfast or a light lunch or supper.

225 g cake flour

2.5 ml salt

5 ml mustard powder

20 ml baking powder

60 g butter or margarine

150 g grated Cheddar cheese

150 ml milk

25 ml milk, for brushing

Preheat the oven to 220 °C.

Coat a baking sheet with cooking spray and set aside. Sift the flour, salt, mustard powder and baking powder into a large mixing bowl. Cut the butter or margarine into the flour and rub in until the mixture resembles breadcrumbs. Stir in the cheese. Make a well in the centre and pour in the 150 ml milk. Mix to form a soft dough. Shape the dough into a ball with the fingers. Turn out onto a lightly floured surface and knead until smooth. Using the hands, press the dough down until 12 mm thick. Using a 7.5 cm floured heart-shaped cutter, cut out the scones and place onto the prepared sheet. Space the scones 2.5 cm apart. Brush the top of each scone with the 25 ml milk and bake for 12–15 minutes or until a skewer inserted into the centre comes out clean. Remove from the oven and turn out onto a wire rack to cool. Serve warm with butter.

# Always-ready Health Muffins

Makes 24

3 jumbo eggs, beaten

400 g (500 ml) golden brown sugar

375 ml cooking oil

200 g bran cereal flakes

700 g cake flour

20 ml baking powder

20 ml bicarbonate of soda

45 ml honey

10 ml salt

1 litre milk

250 g seedless raisins

80 g (250 ml) oats

Preheat the oven to 180 °C.

Coat two 12-hole muffin tins with cooking spray and set aside.

1   Beat together the eggs, brown sugar and oil in a food mixer.

2   Add the remaining ingredients and mix thoroughly.

3   Spoon the batter into the prepared tins, filling each hole halfway.

4   Bake for 25 minutes or until a skewer inserted into the centre comes out clean.

5   Remove from the oven and turn out onto a wire rack to cool.

**Handy hint:** The prepared batter keeps for up to one week in an airtight plastic container in the fridge.

# Apple Oatmeal Muffins
Makes 12

200 ml apple juice

75 ml water

80 g (250 ml) oats

100 g butter or margarine

100 g (125 ml) golden brown sugar

2 jumbo eggs

5 ml vanilla essence

140 g (250 ml) cake flour

5 ml baking powder

5 ml bicarbonate of soda

2.5 ml salt

125 g seedless raisins

Preheat the oven to 180 °C.

Coat a 12-hole muffin tin with cooking spray and set aside. Place the apple juice and water in a small, heavy-based saucepan and bring to the boil. Pour over the oats in a bowl and soak for 15 minutes. Cream the butter or margarine and brown sugar together in a food mixer. Add the eggs, oat mixture and vanilla essence. Sift the cake flour, baking powder, bicarbonate of soda and salt into a bowl and spoon into the batter. Fold in the raisins and mix thoroughly. Spoon the batter into the prepared tin, filling each hole halfway. Bake for 20 minutes or until a skewer inserted into the centre comes out clean. Remove from the oven and turn out onto a wire rack to cool.

**Handy hint:** To keep the tops of the muffins soft, cover with a tea towel during cooling.

# Carrot and Cinnamon Muffins
Makes 6

100 g cake flour

100 g wholewheat flour

80 g (250 ml) oats or wheat bran

1 ml salt

5 ml bicarbonate of soda

45 ml golden brown sugar

5 ml ground cinnamon

75 g (125 ml) seedless raisins

250 ml grated carrots

100 ml cooking oil

75 ml molasses

1 jumbo egg

Preheat the oven to 200 °C.

Coat a six-hole jumbo muffin tin with cooking spray and set aside. Combine the flours, oats or bran, salt, bicarbonate of soda, brown sugar, cinnamon, raisins and carrots in a food mixer. Mix in the oil, molasses and egg, and beat until combined. Spoon the batter into the prepared tin, filling each hole halfway. Bake for 20 minutes or until a skewer inserted into the centre comes out clean. Remove from the oven, leave in the tin for 10 minutes, then turn out onto a wire rack to cool.

# Parmesan Cheese and Chive Muffins

Makes 10

300 g self-raising flour, sifted

20 ml castor sugar

50 g butter or margarine

60 g (250 ml) coarsely grated Parmesan cheese

15 ml mustard powder

75 ml chopped fresh chives

1 jumbo egg

250 ml milk

30 g (125 ml) coarsely grated Parmesan cheese, for sprinkling

Preheat the oven to 190 °C.

Coat a 12-hole muffin tin with cooking spray and set aside. Combine the flour and castor sugar in a large mixing bowl and rub in the butter or margarine until the mixture resembles breadcrumbs. Add the cheese, mustard powder, chives, egg and milk, and mix thoroughly. Spoon the batter into the prepared tin, filling each hole halfway, and sprinkle with the extra cheese. Bake for 25 minutes or until a skewer inserted into the centre comes out clean. Remove from the oven, leave in the tin for 10 minutes, then turn out onto a wire rack to cool.

# Curried Pumpkin Muffins

Makes 6

300 g self-raising flour, sifted

140 g (250 ml) cake flour

5 ml bicarbonate of soda

10 ml castor sugar

10 ml ground cumin

5 ml ground coriander

2.5 ml salt

5 ml curry powder

250 ml cooked, mashed and cooled pumpkin

1 jumbo egg

100 ml cooking oil

250 ml milk

Preheat the oven to 180 °C.

Coat a six-hole jumbo muffin tin with cooking spray and set aside. Combine all the ingredients in a large mixing bowl and stir using a metal spoon until combined. Spoon the batter into the prepared tin, filling each hole halfway. Bake for 20 minutes or until a skewer inserted into the centre comes out clean. Remove from the oven, leave in the tin for 10 minutes, then turn out onto a wire rack to cool.

When making meringues, ensure that the equipment is spotlessly clean and dry. The egg whites need to be completely free of any yolk. Always use eggs that are left at room temperature overnight, ensuring greater volume when whisking. I always make meringues late at night when the oven is free, and on a moisture-free night, as the meringues then dry out properly.

# Meringues Dipped in Chocolate and Walnuts

Makes 24

5 jumbo egg whites

5 ml salt

150 g castor sugar

150 g icing sugar, sifted

10 ml fresh lemon juice

300 g dark chocolate, melted

150 g (250 ml) chopped walnuts

Preheat the oven to 100 °C.

Line two baking sheets with baking paper and set aside. Using an electric beater, beat the egg whites and salt until soft peaks begin to form. Gradually add the castor sugar and icing sugar, beating continuously until stiff peaks begin to form and the mixture becomes glossy. Beat in the lemon juice. Spoon or pipe the meringue onto the prepared sheets and bake for 1 hour. Reduce the oven temperature to 50 °C and bake for a further hour. Switch off the oven and leave the meringues inside for 2 hours with the door closed.

**To assemble:** Dip the base of each meringue into the melted chocolate and then into the walnuts. Place on a wire rack, base side up, to set.

**Handy hint:** Use a little of the prepared meringue to stick the baking paper onto the baking sheet.

# Coffee Meringues with Cappuccino Cream
Makes 26

4 jumbo egg whites

2.5 ml salt

200 g castor sugar

5 ml white wine vinegar

2.5 ml strong instant coffee granules mixed
   to a paste with 2.5 ml boiling water

15 ml cornflour

50 g pecan nuts, toasted
   and coarsely chopped

25 ml maple syrup

5 ml cocoa powder

**Cream Filling**

300 ml fresh cream, whipped

60 ml Greek-style, plain yoghurt

50 g dark chocolate, finely chopped

50 g pecan nuts, toasted and
   coarsely chopped

2.5 ml strong instant coffee granules mixed
   to a paste with 2.5 ml boiling water

Preheat the oven to 110 °C.

Line two baking sheets with baking paper and set aside. Using an electric mixer, beat the egg whites and salt until soft peaks begin to form. Gradually add the castor sugar, beating until stiff peaks begin to form. Add the vinegar, coffee paste and the cornflour. Spoon the meringue onto the prepared sheets and bake for 1 hour. Switch off the oven and leave the meringues inside for 2 hours with the oven door closed.

**To make the cream filling:** Mix together all the ingredients and refrigerate until ready to use.

**To assemble:** Place a meringue onto a serving plate and cover with a dollop of cream. Top with the pecans, drizzle syrup over and lightly dust with cocoa.

# Perfect Pastry

*Whether savoury or sweet, these layers of buttery goodness are always a treat.*

# Preparing Pastry

- Cake flour is always used in pastry making and it is air and not the raising agent that gives the pastry its light texture.
- Work in a cool environment, so that the butter or margarine does not soften or melt.
- Always use fresh, good-quality ingredients to ensure the pastry has a good flavour.
- Measure the ingredients accurately to guarantee a good end result.
- Work quickly and lightly so that the gluten in the flour does not over-develop, as the pastry will become sticky.
- Do not use too much flour on the work surface or the rolling pin, as this will dry out the pastry.
- Roll the pastry lightly and in one direction only, turning frequently – irregular rolling will produce an uneven shape.
- Refrigerating the pastry from time to time will cool it and make it easier to handle.
- Preheating the oven is essential, as the contrast between the heat of the oven and the coolness of the pastry causes expansion of the air trapped in the pastry layers, resulting in a light texture.
- Pastry will keep in the fridge for up to 5 days.
- Pastry freezes well both as a dough and in the made-up form for up to one month.

# Sweet Rich Shortcrust Pastry

Makes 500 g

225 g cake flour

2.5 ml salt

10 ml castor sugar

175 g butter or margarine

1 jumbo egg yolk

10 ml cold water

1  Sift the flour and salt into a large, chilled mixing bowl.

2  Stir in the castor sugar using a metal spoon.

3  Cut the butter or margarine into the flour using a palette knife and rub in lightly with the fingertips until the mixture resembles breadcrumbs.

4  Make a well in the centre and pour in the egg yolk and water.

5  Incorporate the liquid into the mixture using a chilled palette knife.

6  Shape the pastry into a ball, turn out onto a lightly floured surface and knead until smooth.

7  Wrap the pastry in clingfilm and refrigerate for 30 minutes or until ready to use.

# Shortcrust Pastry

Makes 400 g

225 g cake flour
125 g margarine
2.5 ml salt
45 ml cold water

1   Sift the flour into a chilled
    mixing bowl.
2   Rub in the margarine, then add
    the salt and water, and mix.

3   Knead the dough until smooth
    and shape into a ball.
4   Wrap in clingfilm and refrigerate
    for 30 minutes or until ready to use.

# Easy Sweet Tart or Pie Crust Pastry

Makes 250 g

250 g cake flour
1 ml salt

65 g (125 ml) icing sugar
150 g butter or margarine

Sift the flour, salt and icing sugar into a chilled mixing bowl. Rub in the butter or margarine
with the fingertips until the mixture resembles breadcrumbs. Knead the dough until smooth.
Shape the pastry into a ball, wrap in clingfilm and refrigerate until ready to use.

# Flaky Pastry
Makes 350 g

120 g butter
225 g cake flour
2.5 ml salt
10 ml fresh lemon juice
75–100 ml cold water

1. Divide the butter into 4 equal pieces of 30 g each and place on a plate in the fridge.
2. Sift the flour and salt into a chilled mixing bowl.
3. Cut in the first quarter of butter and rub it into the flour with the fingertips.
4. Add the lemon juice and water, and mix to form a soft dough.
5. Turn the pastry out onto a lightly floured surface and knead lightly.
6. Pat the pastry into a rectangular shape and lightly dust a steel rolling pin with flour.
7. Roll out the pastry into an oblong shape using short, light strokes, turning the pastry frequently.
8. Using a palette knife, mark the pastry into three equal sections.
9. Take the second quarter of butter and cut it into small pieces.
10. Dot the butter over the top of two sections of pastry.

11. Fold the unbuttered section of the pastry across the centre section, making sure the ends of the pastry are level.
12. Brush off any surplus flour.
13. Fold the top section of the pastry over the centre section making sure the ends of the pastry are level.
14. Brush off any excess flour.
15. Seal the three edges using a rolling pin and press the pastry at intervals to distribute the air.
16. Wrap the pastry in clingfilm and refrigerate for 20 minutes.
17. Roll out the pastry and repeat steps 7–16 using the third quarter of butter.
18. Fold and roll to seal, then wrap in clingfilm and refrigerate for 20 minutes.
19. Repeat steps 7–16 with the final quarter of butter and refrigerate for at least 30 minutes or until ready to use.

# Puff Pastry

Makes 500 g

225 g cake flour

5 ml salt

120 ml ice-cold water, refrigerated

15 ml fresh lemon juice

225 g unsalted butter

1  Sift the flour and salt into a large, chilled mixing bowl, make a well in the centre and add the water and lemon juice.

2  Mix thoroughly with the fingertips.

3  Shape the pastry into a ball.

4  Turn out onto a lightly floured surface and knead lightly.

5  Wrap the pastry in clingfilm and a damp cloth and refrigerate for 30 minutes.

6  Using a palette knife, shape the butter into a 10 x 15 cm rectangle on a sheet of baking paper.

7  Refrigerate for 15 minutes.

8  Turn the pastry out onto a lightly floured surface and roll out to a 30 cm diameter circle.

9  Position the butter in the centre of the pastry and peel away the paper.

10  Fold the long ends of the pastry over the butter so that the ends overlap.

11  Press gently with the rolling pin or fingertips to seal in the air.

12  Fold the short ends over and seal.

13  If the rectangle of pastry looks misshapen, press it into shape using a palette knife.

14  Turn the pastry so that the long ends are at the top and bottom.

15  Roll out in one direction using light strokes until it is twice its size.

16  Wrap in clingfilm and a damp cloth, and refrigerate for 20 minutes.

17  Turn the pastry out onto a lightly floured surface.

18  Mark three equal sections across the pastry widthwise.

19  Fold the bottom third of the pastry over the centre third and the top third over the top of that.

20  Seal the pastry ends with the rolling pin to seal in the air.

21  Wrap in clingfilm and a damp cloth and refrigerate for 15 minutes. Now the pastry has had one rolling.

22  Turn the pastry out onto a lightly floured surface. The fold should be on the left, the longest sealed end on the right.

23  Roll, fold and refrigerate as before. Repeat this method until the pastry has been rolled and has rested six times.

24  Wrap in clingfilm and a damp cloth, and refrigerate for at least 2 hours or until ready to use.

# Rough Puff Pastry

Makes 225 g

**150 g butter or margarine**
**225 g cake flour**
**2.5 ml salt**
**45 ml cold water**
**10 ml fresh lemon juice**

1 Cut the butter or margarine into small pieces, place on a plate and refrigerate.

2 Sift the flour and salt into a chilled mixing bowl.

3 Add the butter or margarine to the flour and rub in with the fingertips until the mixture resembles breadcrumbs.

4 Add the water and lemon juice and mix to form a soft dough.

5 Turn the pastry out onto a lightly floured surface and shape into a ball. Do not knead.

6 Using short, light strokes, roll the pastry into a 30 x 10 cm rectangle.

7 Turn the pastry so that the long ends are at the top and the bottom.

8 Using a palette knife, mark the pastry into three equal sections.

9 Fold the left third of the pastry over the centre third and the right third over the top of that.

10 Seal the pastry ends with the rolling pin to lock in the air.

11 Roll the pastry to its original size and repeat the folding and sealing.

12 Wrap the pastry in clingfilm and refrigerate for 30 minutes.

13 Repeat the rolling, folding and sealing twice more and, if the pastry is still mottled, roll and fold a fifth time.

14 Refrigerate for at least 30 minutes or until ready to use.

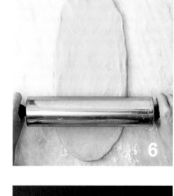

## Quick Puff Pastry
Makes 250 g

| | |
|---|---|
| 250 g cake flour | 15 ml brandy or fresh lemon juice |
| 5 ml salt | 1 jumbo egg yolk |
| 250 g butter, halved | |

Sift the flour and salt into a bowl. Divide between two separate chilled mixing bowls and refrigerate. Remove one bowl from the fridge and, using half the butter, lightly rub into the flour with the fingertips until the mixture resembles breadcrumbs. Mix the brandy or lemon juice and egg yolk in a bowl, add to the flour mixture and mix. Roll the pastry out into a rectangle on a lightly floured surface until 5 mm thick. Take the second bowl from the fridge and rub the remaining butter into the flour until the mixture resembles breadcrumbs. Sprinkle this over the middle third of the rolled-out pastry. Fold the pastry into three, wrap in clingfilm and refrigerate for an hour or until ready to use.

## Cream Cheese Pastry
Makes 250 g

| | |
|---|---|
| 250 g cake flour | 250 g butter or margarine |
| 1 ml salt | 125 g firm, smooth cream cheese |

Sift the flour and salt into a chilled mixing bowl. Cut the butter or margarine into small pieces and rub into the flour with the fingertips until the mixture resembles breadcrumbs. Add the cream cheese and mix. Shape the pastry into a ball, wrap in clingfilm and refrigerate until ready to use.

## Sour Cream Pastry
Makes 350 g

| | |
|---|---|
| 350 g cake flour | 250 g unsalted butter |
| 5 ml salt | 250 ml sour cream |

Sift the flour and salt into a chilled mixing bowl. Cut the butter into small pieces and rub into the flour with the fingertips until the mixture resembles breadcrumbs. Add the sour cream and mix using a palette knife. Shape the pastry into a ball, wrap in clingfilm and refrigerate for 30 minutes or until ready to use.

# Croissants

Makes 44

1 kg cake flour

25 ml white sugar

10 ml salt

1 x 10 g packet instant dry yeast

100 g butter

500 ml milk

2 jumbo eggs

10 ml fresh lemon juice

300 g butter, thinly sliced

1 jumbo egg, beaten, for brushing

**If you have the freezer space, make up as many croissants as needed for the month, then freeze. Remove from the freezer and bake fresh every day.**

Preheat the oven to 200 °C.

Coat baking sheets with cooking spray and set aside.

1   Combine the flour, sugar and salt in a chilled mixing bowl, then add the yeast.

2   Melt the 100 g butter in the milk in a small, heavy-based saucepan, then leave to cool.

3   Add to the dry ingredients together with the eggs and lemon juice, and mix.

4   Knead for 10 minutes or until the dough is smooth and pliable.

5   Wrap in clingfilm and leave to rest for 20 minutes.

6   Turn the pastry out onto a lightly floured surface, knock down and roll out into a rectangle.

7   Cover two-thirds of the pastry with all the slices of butter and fold the unbuttered third over the middle third and the remaining third over the top.

8   Seal the ends and turn the pastry 90°. If necessary, lightly re-flour the surface.

9   Roll the pastry out into a rectangle, fold in three, seal the ends and turn 90°.

10   Wrap in clingfilm and place in the freezer for 20 minutes.

11   Repeat the rolling and folding process four more times, placing in the freezer for 15 minutes each time.

12   Turn the pastry out onto a lightly floured surface and roll out into a 70 x 60 cm rectangle, with the longer end placed horizontally.

13   Using a sharp knife cut the pastry into 4 equal strips widthwise.

14   Mark points 10 cm apart along one side of each strip. Along the other side of the strip, mark points 10 cm apart, starting 5 cm in.

15   Make diagonal cuts between the points to form triangles.

16   Starting at the base, roll up each triangle and place on the prepared baking sheets.

17   Curl the ends into crescent shapes.*

18   Brush with the egg, cover and leave to prove for 30 minutes.

19   Bake for 20 minutes or until golden brown in colour.

*The croissants can be prepared up to this stage, then refrigerated overnight. Remove from the fridge, prove, then bake. Leftover pastry will also keep successfully in the freezer for up to one month, as the cold temperature keeps the yeast dormant.

# Choux Pastry

Makes 24

140 g (250 ml) cake flour
100 g butter or margarine
1 ml salt
300 ml water
4 jumbo eggs, beaten
2.5 ml vanilla essence

Preheat the oven to 200 °C.

Coat baking sheets with cooking spray and set aside.

1  Sift the flour into a mixing bowl.
2  Place the butter or margarine, salt and water into a small, heavy-based saucepan and bring to the boil. Stir continuously with a wooden spoon.
3  Remove the saucepan from the heat and spoon in the flour.
4  Beat until smooth.
5  Return the saucepan to the heat and beat for 1–2 minutes or until the mixture forms a smooth ball.
6  Remove the saucepan from the heat and leave to cool for 3 minutes.
7  Beat in the eggs a little at a time using a wooden spoon.
8  Beat in the vanilla essence.
9  Spoon or pipe the mixture onto the prepared sheets and bake for 20 minutes.
10  Reduce the oven temperature to 190 °C and bake for a further 10 minutes.
11  Once the pastry is cooked, remove from the oven and, using a sharp knife, make a small slit in the side of each pastry, allowing the steam to escape and ensuring the pastry remains crisp as it cools.

The ideal baked choux pastry should be a hollow shell. The more eggs added, the higher and lighter the baked product will be.

# Jam Tarts

Makes 24

1 x quantity Flaky Pastry (see page 166)

120 ml smooth apricot jam

1 jumbo egg white, whisked

25 ml white sugar

Preheat the oven to 220 °C.

Roll the pastry out onto a lightly floured surface until 5 mm thick. Cut into rounds using a floured 7 cm scone cutter. Place a teaspoon of jam into the centre of each pastry round. Fold the rounds in half and seal the ends with a little water. Brush with the egg white and sprinkle with sugar. Place the tarts on ungreased baking sheets and bake for 10 minutes or until golden brown in colour. Remove from the oven and place on a wire rack to cool slightly. Serve warm.

# Old-fashioned Milk Tart

1 x quantity Puff Pastry (see page 168)

**Filling**

4 jumbo eggs, separated

1 litre milk

1 cinnamon stick

piece of naartjie peel

110 g white sugar

70 g (125 ml) cake flour

1 ml salt

50 g butter or margarine

25 ml white sugar mixed with

    2.5 ml ground cinnamon

Preheat the oven to 180 °C.

Coat a 28 cm round pie dish with cooking spray. Line the base and sides of the dish with a thin layer of puff pastry and bake blind (see page 11) for 25 minutes. Set aside to cool.

**To make the filling:** Beat the egg yolks in a bowl and set aside. In a separate bowl, beat the egg whites until stiff peaks begin to form, then refrigerate. Place the milk, cinnamon stick and naartjie peel in a heavy-based saucepan and bring to the boil. Remove from the heat and discard the cinnamon stick and naartjie peel. Mix the sugar, flour and salt in a heatproof bowl and add the hot milk, stirring continuously. Return the mixture to the saucepan and stir over low heat until thick. Remove from the heat, add the butter or margarine and leave to cool slightly. Pour the milk mixture onto the egg yolks, return the mixture to the saucepan and stir over low heat until thick. Remove from the heat and, using a metal spoon, fold in the egg whites. Pour the filling into the prepared pastry shell and bake for 20 minutes. Reduce the oven temperature to 160 °C and bake for 10 minutes. Remove from the oven and sprinkle with the cinnamon sugar mixture. Serve lukewarm or reheat at 180 °C for 15 minutes before serving.

# Yummy Apple Tartlets

Makes 6

250 g butter, softened

180 g castor sugar

5 ml vanilla essence

2 jumbo eggs, beaten

500 g cake flour

2.5 ml salt

**Filling**

50 g butter

5 large Granny Smith or Golden Delicious apples,
    peeled, cored and cubed

50 ml brown sugar

100 g sultanas

100 g dried cranberries

**Topping**

100 g cake flour

5 ml ground cinnamon

2.5 ml ground ginger

60 g butter

80 g brown sugar

8 digestive biscuits, finely crushed

Preheat the oven to 200 °C.

Coat six 13 cm quiche tins with cooking spray and set aside. Cream the butter and castor sugar in a food mixer and beat until light and creamy in colour. Add the vanilla essence and eggs and mix thoroughly. Sift the flour and salt into a bowl and, with the mixer on its lowest speed, add the flour mixture in three or four stages until the mixture resembles breadcrumbs. Using the fingertips, shape the dough into a ball, turn out onto a lightly floured surface and knead lightly until a smooth dough is formed. Wrap in clingfilm and place in the fridge for 30 minutes.

Roll the pastry to 3 mm thick, line the base and sides of the prepared tins and place in the freezer for 10 minutes. Bake blind (see page 11) for 15 minutes, remove from the oven and set aside.

**To make the filling:** Heat the butter in a large, heavy-based pan. Sauté the apples for 5–7 minutes or until golden brown and slightly softened. Stir in the sugar and cook until all the liquid has evaporated. Set aside to cool. Spoon the apples into the pastry bases and scatter over the sultanas and cranberries.

**To make the topping:** Reduce the oven temperature to 180 °C. Sift the flour, cinnamon and ginger into a bowl. Rub in the butter until the mixture resembles breadcrumbs. Stir in the brown sugar and crushed biscuits. Sprinkle the topping over the fruit. Bake the tartlets for 20–30 minutes or until the topping is crisp and golden. Remove from the oven and leave to cool in the tins. Serve with whipped cream and an apple crisp.

# Custard Squares
Makes 18

1 x quantity Sour Cream Pastry (see page 171)

**Filling**
500 ml milk
1 cinnamon stick
30 ml butter or margarine
60 ml white sugar
60 ml custard powder
15 ml cornflour
1 ml salt
4 ml almond essence

**Icing**
130 g (250 ml) sifted icing sugar
10 ml fresh lemon juice
boiling water

Remove the pastry from the fridge and bring to room temperature before rolling to prevent cracking and crumbling. Turn the pastry out onto a lightly floured surface and roll into a 50 x 30 cm rectangle. Mark the centre of the pastry and fold over until the ends meet. Fold in half again. Roll and fold into four once more. Refrigerate for 30 minutes. Remove from the fridge and roll and fold twice more, then refrigerate again for 20 minutes. Preheat the oven to 220 °C. Roll out the pastry on a lightly floured surface and, using a sharp knife, cut into 5 cm squares. Place on an ungreased baking sheet and bake for 10 minutes or until light brown in colour. Turn out onto a wire rack to cool.

**To make the filling:** Heat the milk, cinnamon and butter or margarine in a small, heavy-based saucepan. Remove the cinnamon stick. Combine the sugar, custard powder, cornflour, salt and almond essence in a bowl. Pour the milk into the sugar mixture, return to the saucepan and bring to the boil. Remove from the heat and set aside to cool.

**To make the icing:** Combine the icing sugar and lemon juice in a bowl. Add sufficient boiling water (±5 ml) to make a smooth, glossy, but not watery, icing.

**To assemble:** Split each pastry square horizontally using a sharp knife. Place a teaspoon of filling on the bottom half and cover with the top half of the pastry. Drizzle with the icing.

# Pecan Pie

1 x quantity Sweet Rich Shortcrust Pastry
   (see page 164)
50 g butter or margarine
200 ml golden syrup
1 ml salt
15 ml cake flour
170 g caramel brown sugar
3 jumbo eggs
300 g (750 ml) whole pecan nuts

**Glaze**
200 ml smooth apricot jam

Preheat the oven to 200 °C.

Coat a 28 x 18 cm rectangular loose-based tart tin with cooking spray. Line the base and sides of the tin with the sweet rich shortcrust pastry. Bake blind (see page 11) for 15 minutes, then set aside to cool.

Reduce the oven temperature to 180 °C. Melt the butter or margarine in a small, heavy-based saucepan. Stir in the syrup, salt, flour and sugar, and bring to the boil. Remove from the heat. Beat the eggs in a mixing bowl, pour the syrup mixture into the eggs and stir. Following the shape of the tin, arrange the nuts on the base of the pastry shell and pour the syrup mixture over. Bake for 35 minutes. Remove from the oven and brush the warm pie with the apricot jam.

To melt chocolate successfully, place in an uncovered heatproof bowl over a saucepan of steaming but not boiling water. The water must not touch the base of the bowl. If the chocolate does overheat and becomes lumpy, stir in warm cooking oil a teaspoon at a time until the chocolate is smooth.

## Chocolate Tarts

Makes 6

| | |
|---|---|
| 225 g cake flour | **Filling** |
| 15 ml cocoa powder | 270 g good-quality dark chocolate, melted |
| 2.5 ml salt | 250 ml thick fresh cream |
| 60 g unsalted butter | 50 ml milk |
| 60 g castor sugar | 2 jumbo eggs |
| 1 jumbo egg | 100 g castor sugar |
| 30 g dark chocolate, melted and cooled | 2.5 ml vanilla essence |
| | |
| | 5 ml cocoa powder, for dusting |

Preheat the oven to 190 °C.

Coat six 7 cm round loose-based tart tins with cooking spray and set aside. Sift the flour, cocoa and salt into a mixing bowl. Rub in the butter and add the castor sugar. Add the egg and melted chocolate, and mix with the hands to a smooth pastry. Dust the hands with flour if necessary. Wrap the pastry in clingfilm and refrigerate for 30 minutes. Line the base and sides of the prepared tins with the pastry and refrigerate for 20 minutes. Prick the bases and bake blind (see page 11) for 20 minutes, then set aside to cool.

**To make the filling:** Reduce the oven temperature to 170 °C. Combine all the ingredients in a medium-sized mixing bowl using a balloon whisk. Place the tart tins on a baking sheet and pour in the filling. Bake for 40 minutes. Remove from the oven and leave to cool in the tins for 20 minutes. Cool and dust with cocoa. Serve with ice cream.

# Lemon Tarts with Orange Preserve

Makes 6

**Orange Preserve**

2 oranges, halved and thinly sliced

4 cardamom pods, crushed

1 cinnamon stick

750 ml water

500 g castor sugar

30 ml brandy

**Filling**

3 jumbo eggs

3 jumbo egg yolks

160 g castor sugar

grated rind of 2 lemons

150 ml fresh lemon juice

250 ml thick fresh cream

**Pastry**

250 g cake flour

110 g icing sugar

110 g unsalted butter

1 jumbo egg

**To make the orange preserve:** Place the orange slices in a bowl and cover with cold water. Cover and leave overnight. Drain and place in a large, heavy-based saucepan with the spices and 750 ml water. Bring to the boil, then simmer over low heat for 25–30 minutes or until the orange slices are transparent. Add the castor sugar and cook for 20–25 minutes or until the mixture has a thin, jam-like consistency. Discard the spices, stir in the brandy and set aside to cool.

Preheat the oven to 190 °C.

**To make the pastry:** Coat six 10 cm round loose-based tart tins with cooking spray and set aside. Combine the flour and icing sugar in a food mixer fitted with the plastic blade. Add the butter and process until the mixture resembles breadcrumbs. Add the egg and process until the mixture comes together in a ball. Wrap the pastry in clingfilm and refrigerate for 30 minutes. Line the base and sides of the prepared tins with the pastry and freeze for 10 minutes. Remove the tins from the freezer and bake blind (see page 11) for 10 minutes. Remove from the oven and set aside. Reduce the oven temperature to 175 °C.

**To make the filling:** Combine all the ingredients in a bowl and spoon into the pastry cases. Bake for 20 minutes or until set. Serve at room temperature topped with the orange preserve.

# Yellow Cling Peach Tart

**1 x quantity Easy Sweet Tart or Pie Crust Pastry**
**(see page 165)**

**Filling**

4 large yellow cling peaches, peeled, stoned
    and thinly sliced or 1 x 410 g can
    peach slices, drained
15 ml fresh lemon juice
60 g golden brown sugar
15 ml cake flour
2.5 ml ground cinnamon
5 ml grated lemon rind

**Topping**

100 g butter or margarine, melted
100 g (125 ml) caramel brown sugar
90 g cake flour
60 g wholewheat flour
50 ml pecan nuts, chopped

whipped cream, for serving

Preheat the oven to 180 °C.

Coat a 23 cm round pie dish with cooking spray and line the base and sides with the pastry. Bake blind (see page 11) for 15 minutes and set aside to cool.

**To make the filling:** Combine all the ingredients in a mixing bowl and spoon into the pastry case.

**To make the topping:** Combine all the ingredients in a small bowl and sprinkle the topping over the peach mixture. Bake for 35 minutes and serve warm topped with a dollop of whipped cream.

# Prune and Brandy Tart

1 x quantity Sweet Rich Shortcrust Pastry
   (see page 164)

**Filling**
60 ml brandy
250 g pitted prunes
100 g castor sugar
1 jumbo egg
3 jumbo egg yolks
5 ml vanilla essence
250 ml thin fresh cream

whipped cream, for serving

Preheat the oven to 190 °C.

Coat a 24 cm round loose-based tart tin with cooking spray and line the base and sides with the pastry. Bake blind (see page 11) for 15 minutes and set aside to cool.

**To make the filling:** Place the brandy and prunes in a small, heavy-based saucepan and bring to the boil. Simmer for 1 minute, then remove from the heat and set aside to cool. Drain the prunes, reserving the liquid. Arrange the prunes in concentric circles in the pastry shell. Beat the reserved liquid, castor sugar, egg and yolks and vanilla essence in a mixing bowl. Beat in the cream. Pour the filling into the prepared pastry case and bake for 25–30 minutes or until set. Serve at room temperature topped with a dollop of whipped cream.

# Pink Salmon Choux Puffs

Makes 16

2 x 210 g cans pink salmon, drained and flaked

6 spring onions, chopped

30 ml butter or margarine

1 x 410 g can cream of tomato soup

5 ml salt

1 ml white pepper

6 pickled gherkins, chopped

200 g grated Cheddar cheese

1 x quantity Choux Pastry puffs (see page 174),
    omitting the 2.5 ml vanilla essence

dill sprigs, for garnishing

Preheat the oven to 200 °C.

Sauté the salmon and spring onions in the heated butter or margarine in a small, heavy-based saucepan. Stir in the soup, salt, pepper and gherkins. Bring to the boil. Remove from the heat and stir in the cheese. Set aside to cool.

**To serve:** Slit the baked choux puffs, using a sharp knife. Spoon the mixture into the puffs and heat for 10 minutes on a baking sheet coated with cooking spray. Garnish with dill sprigs.

# Smoked Salmon Quiche

1 x quantity Shortcrust Pastry
    (see page 165)

**Filling**

250 g smoked salmon strips

150 g grated Cheddar cheese

50 ml chopped fresh chives

4 jumbo eggs

250 ml fresh cream

2.5 ml white pepper

15 ml fresh lemon juice

15 ml chopped fresh dill

lemon slices and dill sprigs, for serving

Preheat the oven to 200 °C.

Coat a 28 x 18 cm rectangular loose-based tart tin with cooking spray, line the base and sides with the pastry and bake blind (see page 11) for 10 minutes. Set aside to cool.

Reduce the oven temperature to 160 °C.

**To make the filling:** Arrange the salmon strips on the pastry shell and sprinkle over the cheese and chives. Combine the eggs, cream, pepper and lemon juice in a bowl and pour over the salmon. Bake for 30 minutes and, when cool, sprinkle over the fresh dill. Serve topped with a slice of lemon and a sprig of dill.

# Tamara's Broccoli Pie

**1 x quantity Cream Cheese Pastry (see page 171)**

**Filling**

500 g fresh broccoli florets

6 leeks, sliced

150 g butter or margarine

100 g cake flour

500 ml milk

100 g grated Gruyère cheese

5 ml salt

2.5 ml white pepper

5 ml hot prepared mustard

2 jumbo eggs

15 ml fresh lemon juice

Preheat the oven to 200 °C.

Coat a 35 x 11 cm rectangular loose-based tin with cooking spray, line the base and sides with the pastry and bake blind (see page 11) for 10 minutes. Set aside to cool.

Reduce the oven temperature to 160 °C.

**To make the filling:** Blanch the broccoli in salted boiling water for 15 minutes. Drain and set aside. Sauté the leeks in 50 g butter or margarine in a small heavy-based saucepan, then set aside. Using the same saucepan, melt the remaining butter or margarine, add the flour and stir until cooked. Slowly add the milk and, using a wooden spoon, stir until the sauce thickens. Remove from the heat and stir in the broccoli, cheese and remaining ingredients. Spoon the mixture into the pastry shell and bake for 40 minutes or until cooked.

# Onion and Asparagus Pie

1 x quantity Sour Cream Pastry (see page 171)

**Filling**

3 onions, chopped

30 ml cooking oil

2 jumbo eggs

250 ml milk

1 ml cayenne pepper

2.5 ml salt

100 g grated Cheddar cheese

100 g grated mozzarella cheese

2 x 450 g can asparagus cuts, drained

50 ml chopped fresh chives

Preheat the oven to 200 °C.

Coat a 23 cm round loose-based tart tin with cooking spray, line the base and sides with the pastry and bake blind (see page 11) for 15 minutes. Set aside to cool.

Reduce the oven temperature to 180 °C.

**To make the filling:** Sauté the onions in the heated cooking oil in a heavy-based frying pan and set aside. Beat the eggs, milk, cayenne pepper and salt in a bowl, then set aside. Sprinkle the cheeses and asparagus cuts over the baked pastry shell. Top with the onions and pour the egg mixture over. Sprinkle over the chives and bake for 30 minutes or until set.

# Cheese-filled Pastry Rounds

Makes 20

1 x quantity Puff Pastry (see page 168)

1 jumbo egg, beaten

1 large onion, chopped

30 g margarine

1 x 250 g tub smooth cream cheese

100 g grated Cheddar cheese

5 ml caraway seeds

2.5 ml salt

Preheat the oven to 200 °C.

Coat a baking sheet with cooking spray and set aside. Roll out the pastry on a lightly floured surface until 5 mm thick, and cut into 7 cm rounds. Place a teaspoon of the filling in the centre of a round, brush the edges with the beaten egg and cover with another round. Seal the edges with a fork and brush again with the egg. Place the rounds onto the prepared baking sheet and bake for 15–20 minutes.

**To make the filling:** Sauté the onion in the heated margarine in a small, heavy-based saucepan until transparent, then set aside to cool. Add the remaining ingredients and mix thoroughly.

# Biltong and Palm Heart Quiches

Makes 6

1 x quantity Cream Cheese Pastry (see page 171)

50 g sliced biltong

50 ml chopped fresh parsley

6 leeks, white part only, thinly sliced

30 ml cooking oil

50 g (125 ml) grated biltong

1 x 400 g can palm hearts, drained
    and thinly sliced

100 g grated Cheddar cheese

100 g grated mozzarella cheese

3 jumbo eggs

250 ml fresh cream

125 ml sour cream

2.5 ml salt

1 ml freshly ground black pepper

5 ml mustard powder

15 ml fresh lemon juice

5 ml grated lemon rind

Preheat the oven to 200 °C.

Coat six 10 cm loose-based quiche tins with cooking spray. Line the base and sides with the pastry and bake blind (see page 11) for 10 minutes. Arrange the sliced biltong and parsley on the prepared bases and set aside to cool. Reduce the oven temperature to 180 °C.

**To make the filling:** Sauté the leeks in the oil in a heavy-based frying pan, then set aside. Spoon the leeks, grated biltong and palm hearts into the pastry shells and sprinkle the cheeses over. Mix the remaining ingredients in a bowl and pour over the biltong mixture. Place the quiches on a baking sheet and bake for 20–30 minutes. Serve warm.

If loose-based quiche tins are unavailable, use a 23 cm round pie plate.

# Chicken Vol-au-vents

Makes 8

## Filling

250 ml warm chicken stock

30 ml sago

12 skinless chicken breasts, cut into pieces

2 onions, sliced

60 ml cooking oil

6 peppercorns

2 bay leaves

10 ml salt

150 ml dry white wine

1 jumbo egg yolk

50 ml fresh lemon juice

25 ml chopped fresh parsley

## Pastry

1 x quantity Puff Pastry (see page 168)

1 jumbo egg yolk

**To make the filling:** Pour the stock over the sago in a small bowl and set aside. Sauté the chicken and onions in the heated cooking oil in a medium-sized, heavy-based saucepan. Add the spices, salt, wine and sago. Reduce the heat, cover the saucepan and simmer until tender. Remove the saucepan from the heat and set aside to cool. Stir in the egg yolk, lemon juice and parsley.

Preheat the oven to 220 °C.

**To make the vol-au-vents:** Roll out the pastry 12 mm thick on a lightly floured surface. Using a 10 cm round, floured scone cutter, cut out two pastry rounds. Use a 7 cm round scone cutter or a drinking glass to cut out a small round in the centre of one of the larger rounds. Brush the base of the smaller round with the egg yolk and place onto the bigger round. Repeat with the remaining pastry. Bake the pastry rounds on an ungreased baking sheet for 20 minutes or until cooked. Remove from the oven and set aside to cool.

**To assemble:** Using a sharp knife, cut away the inner circle of the pastry and set aside. Scrape away any soft pastry. Spoon the chicken filling into the vol-au-vents. Top with the smaller pastry rounds. Serve warm.

# Savoury Venison Pies

Makes 3

## Marinade

1 onion, quartered

2 sticks celery, coarsely sliced

6 coriander seeds, crushed

6 whole allspice, crushed

2 bay leaves

2 sprigs parsley

2.5 ml dried marjoram

250 ml dry red wine

100 ml cooking oil

## Filling

1 kg deboned venison, cubed

250 g fresh mushrooms, sliced

30 ml cooking oil

50 ml cake flour

5 ml salt

2.5 ml freshly ground black pepper

## Pastry

1 x quantity Rough Puff Pastry (see page 170)

1 jumbo egg, beaten

**To make the marinade:** Place the venison in a large glass bowl. Combine all the marinade ingredients and pour over. Refrigerate overnight. Remove the venison pieces, strain the marinade and set aside.

Preheat the oven to 220 °C.

**To make the filling:** Sauté the mushrooms in the cooking oil in a heavy-based saucepan until cooked. Add the flour and cook for 1 minute. Stir in the marinade and cook until thick. Add the venison and season with the salt and pepper. Simmer slowly for 1–1½ hours or until tender. Set aside to cool. Spoon the venison into three 13 x 5 cm ceramic dishes.

Roll the pastry to extend 2 cm beyond the edge of the dishes and moisten the edges of the dishes with egg wash. Place the pastry over the top of the dishes, trim the edges and seal. Garnish the tops with pastry cut-outs. Cut a 5 cm cross in the centre of the pastry and open to form a vent. Brush the top of the pastry with the beaten egg. Bake for 15 minutes. Reduce the oven temperature to 190 °C and bake for a further 30 minutes or until the pies are heated through and the pastry is golden brown in colour and crisp. Serve hot.

# Sweet
## *Little Treasures*

*Sugar and spice and all things nice for that special*
*little someone in your life.*

**To ice with ease:** coat the cakes with a thin layer of icing and place in the freezer to harden. Remove and coat the cakes with the remaining icing.

# Kiddies' Parties

- Your child's birthday is the most memorable day of their year. Allowing your child to choose a theme revolving around their current passion gives them a sense of importance. A themed party will be a hit, as children love comparing notes with their friends.
- Parties are part of a happy childhood. Despite all the work, they are a lot of fun, even for the parents.
- Planning ahead is essential – this allows enough time to do everything.
- Setting a budget will help you determine where to spend your money.
- Being creative is easy – a few basic baking tins and these foolproof recipes are all you'll need.
- Party planning is a good time to connect with your child. Involvement in the preparations gives your child a sense of accomplishment.
- Doing the preparations yourself creates excitement – what can be better than the aroma of a home-baked birthday cake?
- The party will be a one-of-a-kind event, providing your child with memories to last forever.

# Birthday Sponge Cake

8 jumbo eggs, separated

4 ml cream of tartar

320 g castor sugar

10 ml vanilla essence

420 g (750 ml) cake flour

2.5 ml salt

15 ml baking powder

200 ml milk

30 ml cooking oil

Preheat the oven to 190 °C.

Coat one 23 cm and one 18 cm square cake tin with cooking spray and set aside. Beat the egg whites and cream of tartar in a food mixer until stiff peaks begin to form. Add the egg yolks one at a time, beating after each addition. Gradually add the castor sugar and beat until the mixture is light and creamy in colour. Add the vanilla essence. Sift the flour, salt and baking powder into a bowl and add alternately with the milk and oil to the egg mixture. Pour the batter into the prepared tins and bake for 45 minutes. Remove from the oven and leave to cool in the tins for 15 minutes. Turn out onto a wire rack to cool. Ice and decorate as preferred.

# Basic Vanilla Cupcakes

Makes 14

140 g (250 ml) cake flour

2.5 ml baking powder

1 ml bicarbonate of soda

1 ml salt

160 g white sugar

90 g butter or margarine, softened

2 jumbo egg whites

5 ml vanilla or almond essence

200 ml buttermilk

Preheat the oven to 180 °C.

Line muffin tins with paper cases and set aside. Sift the flour, baking powder, bicarbonate of soda and salt into a bowl and set aside. Beat the sugar and butter or margarine in a food mixer until the mixture is light and creamy in colour. Add the egg whites one a time, beating well after each addition. Mix in the vanilla or almond essence. Add the flour mixture and buttermilk alternately to the egg mixture and beat until smooth. Spoon the batter into the prepared tins, filling each paper case halfway. Bake for 15–20 minutes or until the tops of the cupcakes spring back when lightly touched. Remove from the oven and leave to cool in the tins for 10 minutes. Turn out onto a wire rack to cool, then ice the cupcakes.

*The Toy Box*

# Oat Buttermilk Teddy Bear Crumpets

Makes 6

 375 ml buttermilk

140 g oats

30 ml honey

1 jumbo egg

1 jumbo egg yolk

60 ml olive oil

75 g self-raising flour

1 ml salt

5 ml ground cinnamon

25 ml cooking oil

2 large bananas

50 g seedless raisins

100 ml honey

Pour the buttermilk over the oats in a mixing bowl and set aside for 10 minutes. Add the honey, egg, egg yolk and oil, and mix thoroughly. Sift the flour, salt and cinnamon into a bowl, then add to the oat mixture. Refrigerate overnight or for at least 2 hours.

**To make the teddy bear crumpets:** Coat a teddy bear-shaped frying pan with the cooking oil and heat. Spoon the batter into the pan and cook until golden brown. Turn over and cook for another minute. Keep the crumpets warm while preparing the remaining batter.

**To serve:** Use sliced banana rounds for the eyes and an angled slice for the mouth. Mark the nose and eyes with a raisin and drizzle the crumpets with honey.

**Handy hint:** If a teddy bear-shaped frying pan is not available, use a heavy-based frying pan and drop in a tablespoon of batter to form the teddy bear's face and two teaspoons of batter to form its ears.

# Baby Blocks
Makes 4

1 x quantity Birthday Sponge Cake batter
(see page 198)

**Icing**
2 x quantities Rich Butter Icing (see page 218)
yellow, green, pink and blue food colouring

**Decoration**
10 x black liquorice laces
200 g white chocolate, melted

Preheat the oven to 180 °C.

Line the bases of two 23 cm square cake tins with baking paper. Coat the tins with cooking spray and set aside. Pour the batter into the prepared tins and bake for 45 minutes or until a skewer inserted into the centre comes out clean. Remove from the oven and leave to cool in the tin for 20 minutes. Turn out onto a wire rack to cool.

**To assemble:** Level the tops of the cakes using a serrated knife. Cut each cake into four squares. Divide the icing amongst four separate mixing bowls and add a different food colouring to each bowl. Using one colour icing, sandwich two of the squares together and coat the top and sides of the squares. Repeat with the remaining three colours. Cut liquorice laces to the required lengths and outline all the edges of the blocks. Pipe melted chocolate numbers and letters onto a sheet of baking paper and set aside. Peel the numbers and letters off the baking paper and place onto the blocks.

Cutters in many different shapes and sizes are available from speciality kitchen shops and department stores. The number of 'friends' you will get from this batch of dough will depend on the size of the cutters used.

## Gingerbread Friends

1 x quantity Perfect Ginger Biscuits dough
   (see page 124)
gingerbread lady and man biscuit cutters

1 x quantity Basic Butter Icing (see page 218)
sweets of different shapes for decoration

Preheat the oven to 190 °C.

Coat a baking sheet with cooking spray and set aside. Place the biscuit dough onto a lightly floured surface and roll out until 5 mm thick. Cut out shapes with the floured cutters. Place the gingerbread shapes onto the prepared sheet and bake for 10–12 minutes or until golden brown in colour. Remove from the oven and turn out onto a wire rack to cool. Sandwich two biscuits together with the butter icing and decorate with the sweets.

## Frankfurter Pastry Envelopes
Makes 24

1 x quantity Rough Puff Pastry (see page 170)
250 ml tomato sauce

12 frankfurters, heated and halved
30 ml sesame seeds

Preheat the oven to 200 °C.

Place the pastry onto a lightly floured surface and roll out until 5 mm thick. Cut the pastry into 7 cm squares and spread with the tomato sauce. Place half a frankfurter in the centre of the pastry square. Sprinkle over the sesame seeds and fold the pastry ends over. Place the pastry envelopes onto an ungreased baking sheet and bake for 25 minutes or until cooked.

## *The Circus*

# Clown Cupcakes

Makes 14

1 x quantity Basic Vanilla Cupcakes batter
   (see page 199)

1 x quantity Basic Butter Icing (see page 218)

ice-cream cones, shortened

marshmallows, halved

Smarties®

jelly sweets

liquorice

small paper doilies

Coat muffin tins with cooking spray. Spoon the batter into the prepared tins, filling each hole halfway. Bake as per the recipe instruction.

**To assemble:** Spread the tops and sides of the cupcakes with the icing. Using the icing, position an ice-cream cone on the top edge of a cupcake as a hat, and position the marshmallows for ears. Use the remaining sweets to form the eyes, nose and mouth, then attach the decorated cupcake with a blob of icing onto a doily as a collar.

# The H-A-P-P-Y B-I-R-T-H-D-A-Y Cupcakes

Makes 16

1 x quantity Basic Vanilla Cupcakes batter
  (see page 199)
red food colouring
1 x quantity Rich Butter Icing (see page 218)
red cord cut into 8 x 20 cm strands, and
  1 x 20 cm strand for 2 bows
red and silver sprinkles

Coat muffin tins with cooking spray. Spoon the batter into the prepared tins, filling each hole halfway. Bake as per the recipe instruction.

**To assemble:** Add the red food colouring to 50 ml icing for the lettering and set aside. Insert a fork into the base of each cupcake to make icing easier and spread the tops with the icing. Pipe the letters onto the cupcakes with the red icing. Position the cord beneath the cupcakes to create the effect of a bunch of balloons. Place the bows in the centre of each 'bunch'. Decorate with red and silver sugar sprinkles.

# Mini Hamburgers with Tomato Sauce
*Makes 20*

1 kg minced beef

2 onions, chopped

2 green apples, cored and grated

150 g (250 ml) seedless raisins

2 slices brown bread, crumbled

7.5 ml salt

1 ml freshly ground black pepper

20 small hamburger rolls

tomato sauce

5 pickled gherkins

Preheat the oven to 160 °C.

Combine all the patty ingredients in a mixing bowl and shape into patties 3 cm in diameter. Place in an oven dish coated with cooking spray and bake for 30 minutes or until cooked.

**To serve:** Cut the rolls in half and toast. Spread with the tomato sauce and top with the hamburger patties. Serve with sliced, pickled gherkins and extra tomato sauce on the side.

# Frozen Yoghurt Ice Creams
*Makes 12*

400 g fresh nectarines, stoned and
    cut into chunks

30 ml golden brown sugar

500 ml low-fat plain yoghurt

12 ice-cream sticks, dipped in food colouring

Coat 12 ice-cream moulds with cooking spray and set aside. Purée the fruit in a food mixer fitted with the metal blade. Add the sugar and yoghurt and mix thoroughly. Spoon the mixture into the prepared moulds and position the ice-cream sticks in the centre. Freeze overnight.

**Handy hint:** Replace the fresh nectarines with 1 x 410 g can sliced peaches, drained, and reduce the sugar to 15 ml.

# The Garden

## Flower Cupcakes
Makes 14

1 x quantity Basic Vanilla Cupcakes batter
   (see page 199)
1 x quantity Rich Butter Icing (see page 218)
paper cupcake cases
marshmallows, sliced into rounds
sugared cake decorations

Coat muffin tins with cooking spray. Spoon the batter into the prepared tins, filling each hole halfway. Bake as per the recipe instruction.

**To assemble:** Spread the tops of the cupcakes with the icing. Place each cupcake into a paper cupcake case. Position the marshmallow slices on the top of the cupcake as petals. Decorate with sugared cake decorations.

# Butterfly Cake

1 x quantity Birthday Sponge Cake batter
   (see page 198)
2 x quantities Basic Butter Icing (see page 218)
lime green, black and pink food colouring
2 x 25 g boxes Smarties®
1 pipe cleaner, halved
template (see page 224)

Preheat the oven to 190 °C.

Coat a deep 30 cm square cake tin with cooking spray. Spoon the batter into the prepared tin and bake for 45 minutes. Remove from the oven and leave to cool in the tin for 20 minutes. Turn out onto a wire rack to cool.

**To assemble:** Enlarge the butterfly template on a photocopier to measure 23 cm in diameter. Place the template on the baked cake, mark out the butterfly with a skewer and, using a sharp knife, cut out the shape. Place 50 ml icing into two separate mixing bowls and colour with the green and black food colouring. Add the pink food colouring to the remaining icing. Spread the pink icing onto the top and sides of the cake. Use the green and black icing and the Smarties® to decorate the cake. Position the pipe cleaners to resemble the antennae.

# Mini Wheat-free Banana Muffins

Makes 24

250 ml cooking oil

6 ripe bananas

120 g caramel brown sugar

110 g (250 ml) oat bran

170 g (250 ml) potato flour

210 g oats

20 ml baking powder

5 ml bicarbonate of soda

10 ml ground cinnamon

2.5 ml mixed spice

Preheat the oven to 180 °C.

Coat a 6.5 cm diameter and a 4 cm diameter 12-hole muffin tin with cooking spray and set aside. Combine the oil, bananas and brown sugar in a food mixer fitted with the metal blade, and mix thoroughly. Add the remaining ingredients and mix until combined. Spoon the batter into the prepared tins, filling each hole halfway. Bake for 40–45 minutes or until a skewer inserted into the centre comes out clean. Remove from the oven and turn out onto a wire rack to cool.

# Mini Smoked Beef Quiches

Serves 12

1 x quantity Cream Cheese Pastry (see page 171)

25 ml chopped fresh parsley

**Filling**

30 ml cooking oil

4 spring onions, chopped

150 g smoked beef, chopped

100 g grated Cheddar cheese

100 g grated mozzarella cheese

3 jumbo eggs

250 ml fresh cream

125 ml sour cream

1 ml salt

1 ml freshly ground black pepper

5 ml mustard powder

15 ml fresh lemon juice

5 ml grated lemon rind

chopped fresh parsley, for garnishing

Preheat the oven to 200 °C.

Coat three 13 cm quiche tins with cooking spray and set aside. Place the pastry onto a floured board and roll out 5 mm thick. Line the quiche tins with the pastry and bake blind (see page 11) for 8–9 minutes. Remove from the oven and sprinkle with the parsley.

**To make the filling:** Reduce the oven temperature to 180 °C. Heat the oil in a heavy-based frying pan and sauté the spring onions and smoked beef. Arrange the beef mixture over the pastry cases and top with the cheeses. Combine the remaining ingredients in a mixing bowl and pour over the smoked beef mixture. Bake for 20–30 minutes. Garnish with the parsley.

*Soccer Fever*

## Star Carrot Cakes

Makes 8

200 g (250 ml) caramel brown sugar

200 ml cooking oil

4 jumbo eggs

210 g (375 ml) cake flour

10 ml baking powder

5 ml bicarbonate of soda

5 ml ground cinnamon

2.5 ml ground ginger

500 ml grated carrots

75 g (125 ml) pecan nuts, chopped

75 g (125 ml) sultanas

250 ml canned crushed pineapple, drained,
    or 250 ml apple sauce

**Cream Cheese Icing**

120 g butter or margarine

500 g icing sugar

5 ml vanilla essence

1 x 250 g tub smooth cream cheese

15 ml fresh lemon juice

5 ml grated lemon rind

silver balls and liquorice sweets

Preheat the oven to 190 °C.

Coat eight 11 cm star-shaped tins with cooking spray and set aside. Beat the brown sugar and oil in a food mixer for 2–3 minutes. Add the eggs and beat thoroughly. Sift the flour, baking powder, bicarbonate of soda, cinnamon and ginger into a bowl and add to the sugar mixture. Add the carrots, nuts, sultanas and pineapple or apple sauce, and mix thoroughly. Spoon the batter into the prepared tins and bake for 25–30 minutes or until a skewer inserted into the centre comes out clean. Remove from the oven and leave to cool in the tins for 10 minutes. Turn out onto a wire rack to cool.

**To make the cream cheese icing:** Cream the butter or margarine in a food mixer and add the icing sugar and vanilla essence. Add the cream cheese, lemon juice and lemon rind, and mix.

**To assemble:** Coat the cakes with the cream cheese icing and decorate with the silver balls and liquorice sweets.

# Soccer Ball Cake

1 x quantity Birthday Sponge Cake batter
   (see page 198)
2 x quantities Rich Butter Icing (see page 218)
100 g liquorice laces
red food colouring
template (see page 224)

**Decorations**

200 g desiccated coconut
5 ml green food colouring
1 x 26 cm and 2 x 16 cm liquorice cables
florist wire

Preheat the oven to 190 °C.

Coat two 18 cm ovenproof glass bowls with cooking spray and set aside. Spoon the batter into the prepared bowls and bake for 55 minutes. Remove from the oven and leave to cool in the bowls for 20 minutes. Turn out onto a wire rack to cool.

**To assemble:** Using a serrated knife, level the tops of the cakes and, using the icing, sandwich the cakes together to form a ball. Ice the outside of the cake. Using a 4 cm diameter hexagon template, mark out the hexagons on the cake with the liquorice. Add the food colouring to the remaining icing and coat every alternate hexagon shape red.

**To make the grass and goal post:** Colour the coconut with the green food colouring and sprinkle it around the cake. For the goal post, cut the liquorice into the required lengths and insert the florist wire into the centre of the cables (warn children not to eat this).

To mark the hexagonal shapes on the icing,

use a tracing wheel dipped in cocoa powder.

# Award-winning Rosettes

Makes 30

2 x 200 g packets Marie biscuits or
    plain, sweet, round biscuits
1 x quantity Basic Butter Icing
    (see page 218)

30 white marshmallows, sliced into
    rounds and halved
red food colouring
strings of sweet necklaces

Coat the biscuits with the icing and position the slices of marshmallow around the outer edge. Add the food colouring to the remaining icing and pipe with '1st'. Attach the sweet necklaces to the rosettes using the remaining icing.

# Focaccia Fingers

Serves 10–12

75 ml olive oil
375 ml lukewarm water
1 x 10 g packet instant dry yeast
140 g (250 ml) white bread flour
350 g (625 ml) white bread flour

20 ml olive oil
10 ml salt
7.5 ml coarse salt
25 ml chopped fresh rosemary

Preheat the oven to 200 °C.

Coat a 37 x 26 cm baking sheet with 25 ml of the 75 ml olive oil and set aside. Combine the water and yeast in a food mixer fitted with the dough hook and set aside until frothy. Mix in the 140 g bread flour to make a soft smooth batter. Cover the bowl with clingfilm and leave the batter to rise in a warm place until it is thick and foamy and nearly doubled in size. Add the 350 g bread flour, 20 ml olive oil and salt. Mix and knead the dough with the dough hook on medium speed for about 10 minutes or until smooth and pliable. Transfer the dough to a bowl lightly oiled with another 25 ml of the 75 ml olive oil. Turn to coat, cover with clingfilm and leave to rise in a warm place until nearly doubled in size. Fold the dough over by lifting the ends up and over the centre. Cover with clingfilm and set aside for 15 minutes.

Dust the surface lightly with flour. Turn the dough out and, using the palms, gently stretch the dough into a rectangle 2.5 cm thick and nearly the same dimensions as the baking sheet. Transfer to the prepared baking sheet. Cover with clingfilm and let the dough rise until it springs back to the touch. Use the fingertips to dimple the surface of the focaccia and drizzle with the final 25 ml olive oil. Sprinkle with the coarse salt and rosemary. Bake for 30 minutes or until the focaccia has a golden brown crust and sounds hollow when tapped underneath. Turn out onto a wire rack to cool. Cut into fingers and serve.

# Fabulous
# Frosting

*These delectable toppings will prove
to be the icing on any cake.*

# Rich Butter Icing
Makes 500 ml

450 g icing sugar
200 g butter, softened
5 ml vanilla essence

Beat the icing sugar and butter in a food mixer until creamy. Add the vanilla essence and beat until smooth. Spoon into a container and set aside until ready to use.

# Basic Butter Icing
Makes 500 ml

450 g icing sugar
100 g butter
5 ml vanilla essence
45 ml milk

Cream the icing sugar and margarine in a food mixer until creamy. Add the vanilla essence and milk and beat until smooth. Spoon into a container and set aside until ready to use.

Only use butter and milk kept at room temperature.

For best results only ice or sandwich cakes together that have

been cooled to room temperature.

Use a palette knife or spatula to spread the icing onto the cake.

# American Frosting

Makes 500 ml

2 jumbo egg whites

1 ml cream of tartar

100 ml cold water

300 g icing sugar

1 ml salt

15 ml honey or golden syrup

5 ml vanilla essence

Combine all the ingredients except the vanilla in the top of a double boiler over simmering water and beat with a hand beater until blended, then continue beating until the mixture holds its shape and stiff peaks begin to form. Remove from the heat and pour into a large bowl. Add the vanilla essence and continue beating until the frosting has cooled and the mixture is very stiff. Set aside until ready to use.

**Handy hint:** To measure the honey or syrup with ease, warm the spoon in boiling water, dry and use immediately.

# Ganache

Makes 500 ml

250 ml thin fresh cream

300 g dark chocolate, broken into pieces

100 g unsalted butter, softened

Place the cream in a small, heavy-based saucepan, bring to the boil and immediately remove from the heat. Place the chocolate in a small bowl, pour half the cream over and stir thoroughly. Add the remaining cream and stir until smooth. Add the butter and stir until combined. Cover and leave in a cool place for 1 hour or until thickened. Do not refrigerate.

# Glossary

**Bake blind:** Baking a pastry case before filling it. The uncooked pastry is lined with baking paper and filled with dried beans or uncooked rice to prevent it rising.

**Baking powder:** Raising agent consisting of two parts cream of tartar to one part bicarbonate of soda.

**Batter:** An uncooked mixture of flour, liquid and a raising agent such as baking powder.

**Beat:** Rapidly combine ingredients using electric beaters, a rotary beater or a wooden spoon.

**Bicarbonate of soda:** A component of baking powder. It acts as a raising agent when combined with cream of tartar.

**Biltong:** Dried strips of spiced beef or game.

**Blanching:** Immersing fruit or vegetables in boiling water for a short period and then in iced water.

**Bread flour:** Also known as strong flour.

**Butter:** The most commonly used fat for cake making, as it creams well and has the best flavour.

**Butter, salted:** Has two per cent salt added.

**Butter, unsalted:** Best for use in baking.

**Buttermilk:** Made by adding a culture to skim milk and leaving the mixture to sour and thicken.

**Cake flour:** Also known as plain flour.

**Cornflour:** Fine white powder made from maize or wheat. Used in small quantities in sponge cakes or shortbread to produce a lighter texture.

**Cream together:** Beating butter and sugar until light and creamy. Electric beaters or a rotary beater can be used.

**Dough:** A thick mixture of flour and liquid.

**Dried currants:** Tiny, almost-black raisins.

**Dust:** Cover lightly with icing sugar or cocoa powder that is sifted over the top of a cake or tart prior to serving.

**Egg wash:** Beaten egg brushed over dough or pastry to give a shine when baked.

**Fold:** Using a gentle motion to incorporate air into the mixture.

**Fruit cake mix:** Combination of sultanas, raisins, currants, mixed citrus peel and cherries.

**Ganache:** A dark chocolate and cream mixture for filling or coating cakes.

**Glacé fruit:** Fruit that is preserved in sugar.

**Glaze:** Beaten egg, egg white or milk painted over cakes or pastries to give a glossy appearance. Syrup or jam is used to glaze tarts.

**Granadilla:** Also known as passionfruit.

**Jam:** Whole ripe fruit that is cooked to a pulp with sugar until it sets.

**Knead:** Work dough with the hands on a flat, floured surface. The dough is punched to develop the gluten in the flour.

**Mascarpone:** Fresh, thick cream cheese with a delicately sweet, slightly acidic flavour.

**Meringue:** Stiffly beaten egg whites and sugar, baked until cooked.

**Mix:** Combining two or more ingredients.

**Mixed citrus peel:** Also known as candied citrus peel.

**Mixed spice:** Combination of ground cinnamon, allspice and nutmeg.

**Pastry:** Dough made from a combination of flour, butter and liquid.

**Pipe:** Meringue, icing or whipped cream forced through a piping bag fitted with a nozzle.

**Prove or Proving:** Last rising before the baking process, and the shaping of the dough and leaving it to rise on a baking sheet until doubled in size before baking.

**Punch down:** Yeast dough is punched down after the first rising, shaped and left to rise for a second time.

**Rest:** Batter or dough set aside to allow the gluten to develop.

**Rind:** Outer layer of all citrus fruit.

**Rub in:** Combining flour and butter or margarine with

the fingertips until the mixture resembles breadcrumbs.

**Self-raising flour:** Cake flour sifted with baking powder in the proportion of 250 ml flour to 10 ml baking powder.

**Sift:** Aerate a dry ingredient through a sieve to remove lumps.

**Sugar, caramel:** Soft, fine granulated sugar containing molasses to give it its characteristic colour.

**Sugar, castor:** Finely granulated table sugar.

**Sugar, golden brown:** Coarse, granulated yellow sugar.

**Sugar, icing:** Confectioner's sugar.

**Sugar, white:** Coarse, granulated table sugar.

**Sultanas:** Dried, seedless white grapes.

**Syrup, golden:** Thick, sticky syrup with a deep golden colour.

**Syrup, maple:** Light brown syrup made from the sap of the maple tree.

**Vanilla essence:** Distilled from the seeds of the vanilla pod.

**Vol-au-vent:** Small round case of puff pastry filled with a savoury mixture.

**Whisk:** Beating with a light, rapid movement using a whisk.

**Yeast, fresh:** Raising agent, which is blended with water to form a smooth cream, added to liquids and left to foam before being added to the dry ingredients.

**Yeast, instant dried:** Raising agent, which is packaged and added to liquid or mixed directly into the dry ingredients.

## Oven Temperatures

| °C (Celsius) | °F (Fahrenheit) | Gas Mark |
|---|---|---|
| 100 °C | 200 °F | ¼ |
| 110 °C | 225 °F | ¼ |
| 120 °C | 250 °F | ½ |
| 140 °C | 275 °F | 1 |
| 150 °C | 300 °F | 2 |
| 160 °C | 325 °F | 3 |
| 180 °C | 350 °F | 4 |
| 190 °C | 375 °F | 5 |
| 200 °C | 400 °F | 6 |
| 220 °C | 425 °F | 7 |
| 230 °C | 450 °F | 8 |
| 240 °C | 475 °F | 9 |

## Quick Conversions

| | ¼ cup (60 ml) | ½ cup (125 ml) | ¾ cup (200 ml) | 1 cup (250 ml) |
|---|---|---|---|---|
| Cake flour | 35 g | 70 g | 105 g | 140 g |
| White/brown bread flour | 35 g | 70 g | 105 g | 140 g |
| White/brown sugar | 50 g | 100 g | 150 g | 200 g |
| Castor sugar | 52 g | 105 g | 160 g | 210 g |
| Icing sugar | 35 g | 65 g | 100 g | 130 g |
| Cocoa powder | 25 g | 50 g | 75 g | 100 g |
| Butter/margarine | 60 g | 115 g | 175 g | 230 g |
| Raisins/currants | 40 g | 75 g | 115 g | 150 g |
| Nuts, whole | 25 g | 50 g | 75 g | 100 g |
| Nuts, chopped | 37.5 g | 75 g | 112.5 g | 150 g |

## Conversion Charts

| Metric | US Cups | Imperial |
|---|---|---|
| 1 ml | ¼ tsp | – |
| 2.5 ml | ½ tsp | – |
| 4 ml | ¾ tsp | – |
| 5 ml | 1 tsp | ³⁄₁₆ fl oz |
| 15 ml | 1 Tbsp | ½ fl oz |
| 25 ml | 5 tsp | 1 fl oz |
| 50 ml | 3 Tbsp + 1 tsp | 1¾ fl oz |
| 60 ml | 4 Tbsp/¼ cup | 2 fl oz |
| 80 ml | ⅓ cup | 2¾ fl oz |
| 125 ml | ½ cup | 4 fl oz |
| 200 ml | ¾ cup | 7 fl oz |
| 250 ml | 1 cup | 9 fl oz |
| | | |
| 25 g | – | 1 oz |
| 50 g | – | 2 oz |
| 75 g | – | 3 oz |
| 100 g | – | 4 oz |
| 150 g | – | 5 oz |
| 200 g | – | 7 oz |
| 250 g | – | 9 oz |
| 500 g | – | 1 lb 2 oz |
| 750 g | – | 1 lb 10 oz |
| 1 kg | – | 2 lb 4 oz |

# Index